On an Ungrounded Earth:
Towards a New Geophilosophy

ON AN UNGROUNDED EARTH

TOWARDS A NEW GEOPHILOSOPHY

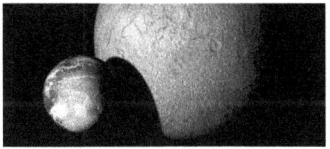

Ben Woodard

punctum books ✶ brooklyn, ny

 ON AN UNGROUNDED EARTH: TOWARDS A NEW GEOPHILOSOPHY
© Ben Woodard, 2013.

http://creativecommons.org/licenses/by-nc-nd/3.0

This work is Open Access, which means that you are free to copy, distribute, display, and perform the work as long as you clearly attribute the work to the authors, that you do not use this work for commercial gain in any form whatsoever, and that you in no way alter, transform, or build upon the work outside of its normal use in academic scholarship without express permission of the author and the publisher of this volume. For any reuse or distribution, you must make clear to others the license terms of this work.

First published in 2013 by
punctum books
Brooklyn, New York
http://punctumbooks.com

ISBN-13: 978-0615785387
ISBN-10: 0615785387

Cover Image: computer fractalization of detail from Ernst Haeckel (1834-1919), *Kunstform der Natur* (1904), plate 70: organisms classified as Ophiodea.

Facing-page drawing by Heather Masciandaro.

for K., my accomplice at the abyss's edge

Acknowledgments

While much of this book was written in solitude, the ideas on which it rests, as always, belong to others. I am especially grateful for the work of Iain Hamilton Grant and Reza Negarestani, whose brilliance completely restructured my own thinking and, as a result, many of their ideas occupy the core of this text. I wish to thank my classmates and professors during my time at the European Graduate School where I first began this project. I also wish to thank all those who have continually surprised and humbled me with their interest in this book throughout its plodding formation.

Lastly, I must thank Eileen Joy for her perpetual support and tireless efforts, as well as Nicola Masciandaro for his editorial toil. Most of all, I must thank Andrew Weiss for his uncanny thoroughness and care in editing and commenting on this manuscript. It is to him I owe more than I can repay for helping me to bring this book into material existence.

Table of Contents

0 | Introduction, or, Abyss Lessons   1

1 | Wormed Earths, or, Abyssal Ungroundings and Torsional Porosities   5

    1.1. The Earth is a Living Island
    1.2. Schelling's Unground
    1.3. Decay
    1.4. Worms, or, Internal Ungrounding

2 | External Ungroundings   27

    2.1. Externality as Spatial Torsion
    2.2. Digging Machines
    2.3. Planet Demolishing
    2.4. A Brief Note on Directionality

3 | Regroundings   47

    3.1. Xenoarchaeology
    3.2. Strange Temporalities
    3.3. Internal and External Potentialities
    3.4. The Organic/Inorganic Blur
    3.5. Geocontainment, or, The Panic of Burial

4 | Hell Dimensions 71

    4.1. Hell In (>), or, Infernology as Geophilosophy
    4.2. Volcanic Orifices
    4.3. Against Over-Demonization
    4.4. Hell Out (<)

5 | To Conclude, or, A Dark Earth, A Black Sun 83

    5.1. Dark Earth
    5.2. Black Sun

Excursus: Nihilismus Autodidacticus 93

Bibliography 97

0. INTRODUCTION, OR
ABYSS LESSONS

The geophilosopher is one who philosophically experiences rather than flees the earth, who passes through by remaining with it. Geophilosophical experience entails facing, more and more deeply, the fact of earth as the place of philosophy, and more profoundly, experiencing earth as facticity itself, the site of thought's passage to the absolute.
                      Nicola Masciandaro, "Becoming Spice"

Thinking takes place in the relationship of territory and the earth.
                      Deleuze and Guattari, *What is Philosophy?*

In Jules Verne's *Journey to the Center of the Earth*, Professor Lidenbrock, after exploring the town of Grauben, forces his nephew up the narrow staircase of a church in order to induce vertigo. The professor tells him that they must take "abyss lessons,"[1] in order to prepare themselves for their forthcoming descent into the planet. In the spirit of Deleuze and Guattari's appropriation of Sir Arthur Conan Doyle's Professor Challenger, what we require is the services of a geophilosopher (or

---

[1] Jules Verne, *Journey to the Center of the Earth* (New York: Bantam Classic, 2006), 42.

geophysicist), possessed with the madness of Lidenbrock, in order to unground the earth in philosophical and folk thinking.

In far too much continental philosophy, the Earth is a cold dead place enlivened only by human thought—either as a thing to be exploited, or as an object of nostalgia. This split is endemic to philosophies of nature on the whole, a split diagnosed by Pierre Hadot as the divide between the Promethean and Orphic tendencies in viewing nature. Furthermore, this divide not only presents a false choice between exploitative capitalist Cartesianism and neo-pagan Spinozism, but also wrongfully presupposes that nature is a thing ontologically separate from humanity. That is, both the Promethean and the Orphic tendencies assume that human beings are *a priori* set apart from nature, either due to divine entities (God, Soul, etc.) or to our purportedly unique cognitive abilities.

Setting aside religious arguments for the sake of realism and materialism (and brevity), the Earth has been used to ground thought instead of bending it; such grounding far too often gives too much supposedly immovable ground to thinking, leaving the planet as nothing but a stage for phenomenology, deconstruction, and other forms of anthropocentric philosophy. Geophilosophy, to return to Deleuze and Guattari, is named as the invention of Nietzsche,[2] and, as Masciandaro notes, after Nietzsche geo-philosophy devolves into a philosophy of place (*topos*),[3] particularly in Heideggerian philosophy, as the earth is carved into dwellings, homes, and the open.[4]

While there have been some attempts at showing how the earth-as-process is integral to humanity's existence, such

---

[2] Gilles Deleuze and Félix Guattari, *What is Philosophy?* trans. Graham Burchell and Hugh Tomlinson (London: Verso, 1994), 85.
[3] Nicola Masciandaro, "Becoming Spice: Commentary as Geophilosophy," *COLLAPSE* VI: Geo/Philosophy (January 2010): 33 [20–56].
[4] Masciandaro, "Becoming Spice," 34–35.

as Manuel De Landa's discussion of *Homo sapiens*' endoskeletons as mineral invasion,[5] or Jane Bennett's ecopolitics, the terrestrial globe on which we haplessly crawl begs for more philosophical attention, especially as the globe has contoured every aspect of our material, cultural, and noetic existence.

This will be our task.

---

[5] Manuel De Landa, *A Thousand Years of Nonlinear History* (Cambridge: Zone Books, 2000), 27.

1. WORMED EARTHS, OR, ABYSSAL UNGROUNDINGS AND TORSIONAL POROSITIES

> Although solidus, or the ground, with its gravity, integrity and tyrannical wholeness is ultimately restrictive, the eradication of the ground also results in the rise of another hegemonic regime—the regime of death and destruction.... Ungrounding is involved with discovering or unearthing a chemically-degenerating underside to the ground.
> Reza Negarestani, *Cyclonopedia*

> The infrastructure of the terrestrial process inheres in the obstructive character of the earth, in its mere bulk as a momentary arrest of solar energy flow.
> Nick Land, *Thirst for Annihilation*

1.1. THE EARTH IS A LIVING ISLAND

In one of their many plateaus, Deleuze and Guattari subject the earth (in both meanings of the term—to affect and to subjugate), through the recapitulated figure of Professor Challenger, to pain. They torture our home planet to reveal its secrets, thereby solidifying their codification of the earth as a "who" and not an "it." This harkens back to Aristotle's tetrasomia or Kant's image of nature as geosomatic, in which the earth becomes something corporeal that can be tied to the rack and then stretched for her secrets. Our concern here is slightly different. As Iain Hamilton Grant points out in *Philosophies of Nature After Schelling*, Kant's own somatization of the earth operates via a crypto-Aristotelianism. For Aristotle, physics must always be a "science of the body."[6] As Grant points out in the closing chapters, Deleuze is complicit in this somaphilia, which reduces nature to a collection of objects, wherein the earth becomes a place or set of places, instead of a materially vital life/thought engine.

This is to say nothing of Husserl's ark-ization of the earth (the earth as the "original ark," where the Earth is flung back in time to its pre-Copernican state as merely the bounds of experience), as over-romanticized ground (*Boden*), or of what Heidegger would call *Offenheit*, or openness, as Meleau-Ponty shows.[7] It is such images of Earth as both dead body and mute cradle that we set out to destroy with digging machines, massive energy weapons, and total ecological collapse. These images perform a dual criminal function: one, to stabilize thinking, and two, to give gravity to anthropocentric thinking and being.

The earth-anchoring of thought has a long tradition. In his study of Bataille, Nick Land writes, "A dark fluidity at the roots of our nature rebels against the security of *terra firma*, provoking a wave of anxiety in which we are submerged."[8] Through the oceanic metaphor Land demonstrates how the auto-binding of thought to Earth caricatures both. This oceanic thinking leads us to the image of the island (which functions as a liminal point between the terrestrial and the aquatic), a common element in philosophical texts. The island stretches from Ibn Tufayl's *Philosophus Autodidactus*, to

---

[6] Iain Hamilton Grant, *Philosophies of Nature After Schelling* (London: Continuum, 2006), 31.

[7] Maurice Merleau-Ponty, *Nature: Course Notes from the College de France* (Evanston: Northwestern University Press, 2003), 77.

[8] Nick Land, *The Thirst for Annihilation: Georges Bataille and Virulent Nihilism* (London: Routledge, 1992), 107.

Plato's Atlantis, to Bacon's Atlantis, to Kant's island of truth in the *Critique of Pure Reason*, all the way to Deleuze's desert islands. Outside philosophical texts, one hardly need mention the television series *Lost* and its population of characters named after philosophers.

Lost is just one of the more recent examples of the long metaphoric use of islands, a use which Milan Cirkovic explores, in his essay "Sailing the Archipelago":

> We live on a small island. We have not yet ventured much beyond our immediate locale on this small island; even our own inconspicuous location still holds great mysteries for us. It seems that we find ourselves near the mountain peak of our island, but even that is uncertain. We have only recently discovered that there are other islands besides our home scattered in a vast (possibly infinite) ocean. And the ocean is dead."[9]

The idea of the earth as an island reinforces the fact that the earth is not bounded in a well-defined way, nor is it immune to the rages of the ocean and other forces—radiation, cosmic rays, meteorites and so on. Cirkovic defines an island as "a set of parameters describing habitable universes which are close in parameter space."[10] He thus denaturalizes the earth, making it a particular parameter of nature and not an automatically stable philosophical given.

Here we wish to subject the earth to pain—not as a somatized creature, but as a planet, the glob of baked matter that it is—in order to test its limitropic porosity and see how much ungrounding the earth can take before it ceases to be simultaneously an example of nature's product and also its

---

[9] Milan Cirkovic, "Sailing the Archipelago," *COLLAPSE* V: The Copernican Imperative (February 2009): 293.

[10] Cirkovic, "Sailing the Archipelago," 297.

productivity. The digging or ungrounding of the earth is often tied to thought, as the work of depth is a digging that occurs, to borrow Deleuze's phrase, in the image of thought. For Deleuze, thought does all the digging: dynamism is contained within the idea.[11] This is unfortunate given the following passage:

> There is necessarily something cruel in this birth of a world which is a chaosmos, in these worlds of movements without subjects, roles without actors. When Artaud spoke of the theater of cruelty, he defined it only in terms of an extreme 'determinism,' that of spatio-temporal determination in so far as it incarnates an Idea of mind or nature. . . . Spaces are hollowed out, time is accelerated or decelerated, only at the cost of strains and displacements which mobilise and compromise the whole body.[12]

Again, the specter of somatization returns. Furthermore, Deleuze's virtualization of the idea guarantees a pre-thinkability of nature in-itself: a necessary move given Deleuze's denial of transcendence and his valorization of the univocity of being, or singular ontology.[13]

Against such somatization and over-ideation of nature and the Earth, Iain Hamilton Grant argues that the dyad of producer and produced disappears via the cosmic striations of matter over time, and yet, the retroactive recognition of mammalian perception digs objects out of the flatness of time as if they were static, thereby orienting them to our attempts to make sense of time, a time-for-us. One must, against correlationist *doxa* (where the universe is only understood in

---

[11] Deleuze, *Difference and Repetition*, trans. Paul Patton (New York: Columbia University Press, 1994), 218–219.

[12] Deleuze, *Difference and Repetition*, 219.

[13] Deleuze, *Difference and Repetition*, 35.

relation to human frames of perception) take the weight of the cosmic cascade into the pulsations of everyday life as saturating the seen and unseen. This requires a certain inaccessibility regarding the materiality/reality of existence (thereby shattering any all-encompassing univocity/immanence) as well as a redefinition of the transcendental to appease such inaccessibility. This task is assisted by differentiating Deleuze's use of ground from Schelling's, through the transmogrification of the transcendental.

As Grant indicates, Schelling's ground and process of ungrounding moves against the Kantian/Fichtean privileging of world over earth.[14] While it would seem that Deleuze combats this move, his thinkable (inter-ideal) differentiation-as-transcendence departs significantly from Schelling. Grant writes: "the nature of the Schellingian transcendental is, as we have seen, as different from the Deleuzian as from the Kantian: the earth itself, as a productive product, is to that extent a natural transcendental or a *Scheinprodukt*."[15] Where Deleuze somatizes nature, Schelling searches for the unthinged.[16]

1.2. SCHELLING'S UNGROUND

Grant's resuscitation of Schelling's transcendental geology functions to realize Schelling's ground by developing a realism (i.e., Schelling's idealism remains qualified by nature), whereas by contrast, "Deleuze maintains the antithesis of nature and freedom, and thus does not determine the one by the other ... at the cost of regionalizing matter with respect to ideation."[17] As Grant continues, this line of thinking brings Deleuze close to his nemesis Hegel, in that both seem to deny how geology

---

[14] Grant, *Philosophies of Nature,* 199–200.

[15] Grant, *Philosophies of Nature,* 201.

[16] Grant, *Philosophies of Nature,* 165.

[17] Grant, *Philosophies of Nature,* 202.

could affect thought.[18]

The transcendental geology of Schelling not only redefines the transcendental as the capacity for the unknown to seize thought, and to produce thought and thought's necessary material ground, but also redefines the temporal quality of all actualization.[19] The central concern for Grant in regards to Schellingian anteriority is what he calls powers—a concern that Deleuze recognizes but then seems to forget.[20] The importance of a powers-ontology lies in the fact that any object cannot contain its own conditions for coming to be that object, whether that object be an idea, a terrestrial sphere, or a perforation of that sphere. Hegel's world of eternal becoming, like Deleuze's world-as-egg, denies actuality its temporality—hence Hegel's and Deleuze's rejection of realist geology.[21]

Grant summarizes the importance of such a geology in the following way:

> If geology, or the 'mining process,' opens onto an ungroundedness at the core of any object, this is precisely because there is no 'primal layer of the world', no 'ultimate substrate' or substance on which everything ultimately rests. The lines of serial dependency, stratum upon stratum, that geology uncovers do not rest on anything at all, but are the records of *actions* antecedent in the production of consequents.[22]

The mechanics of ungrounding, however, cannot be reduced to anteriority in either its physical or ideal forms. If

---

[18]Iain Hamilton Grant, "Mining Conditions," in *The Speculative Turn: Continental Materialism and Realism*, eds. Levi Bryant, Nick Srnicek and Graham Harman (Melbourne: re.press, 2010), 41–46.
[19]Grant, "Mining Conditions," 44.
[20]Deleuze, *Difference and Repetition,* 190.
[21] See Grant, "Mining Conditions."
[22]Grant, "Mining Conditions," 44.

we hold to a powers-ontology, then the process of grounding and ungrounding must be articulated in the most base articulation of powers, that of spatio-temporality. This spatio-temporality is a simultaneous ungrounding/grounding and interiorizing/exteriorizing. As Ray Brassier notes in his text "Concepts and Objects," such dualities are not outmoded metaphysical baggage, but are necessary, especially given the troubling indistinction of ontology and epistemology once anthropocentric veils have been torn.[23]

While Schelling is easily the master of grounding and ungrounding, we will have to look elsewhere to develop a theory of interiority/exteriority and the relation of the two terms to one another. Michael Vater points out that Schelling's utilization of temporality as the individuating factor in his identity philosophy leads to an opposition of the internal and external that is far too simplistic.[24] However, this claim denies the naturephilosophical concerns of Schelling, according to which the real is connected with externality, while this externality is separated from the internality of the mind only formally and not qualitatively. Schelling's philosophy has frequently been disregarded as a step towards Hegel, as failing to extend or transform Kant in the degree which Fichte and Hegel did—the former exacerbating the ego to an extreme positivity, the latter intensifying the I in a negative sense in order to overcome the being/knowing balancing act of Kant. To see Schelling in this way is to see him as far more Kantian than he is. Schelling, then, must be thoroughly spatialized. In one of Grant's many Schellingian adventures, he comments on the disregard of interiority when it comes to temporal expansion.[25]

---

[23]Ray Brassier, "Concepts and Objects," in *The Speculative* Turn, eds. Bryant, Srnicek, and Harman, 47–65.

[24]F.W.J. Schelling, *Bruno, or, On the Natural and Divine Principle of Things*, trans. Michael G. Vater (New York: State University of New York Press, 1984), 76, 78.

[25]Ray Brassier, Iain Hamilton Grant, Graham Harman, and Quentin

Interiority becomes problematic from a point of view of realism, as it cannot merely be a temporal distinction; temporal distance cannot determine the reality of objects, of their inaccessibility. That is, time alone cannot explain the layering of the world; there must be a materiality which is not merely formal. Space suffers a similar problem (perhaps unsurprisingly, given the logical interdependence of time and space) as, at its deepest ground, it blurs the distinction between base materiality and pure formalism. Or, in other words, space cannot be taken as merely the stage of matter.[26] It is a quality of gravity[27] that controls the motion of matter and is warped by matter in kind.[28] This brings us back to Schelling's powers and how the interaction of powers can be called a materialism, materiality, or perhaps, realism.

1.3. EXAGGERATED DECAY

Two theorists will aid us in the project of a realist and truculent theory of space-time as non-formal and generative: Reza Negarestani and Martin Hägglund.

Reza Negarestani further destructs the Deleuzo-Guattarian terrestrial determination by investigating the poromechanics of the Earth: the vital but non-vital work of decay, hollowing out life, where "[t]he cosmogenesis of decay unfolds within solidity, [and] spreads from interior to outer surfaces."[29] These intrinsic temporal dimensions are brought out explicitly in Negarestani's "*Memento Tabere*: Reflections

---

Meillassoux, "Speculative Realism," *COLLAPSE* III: Unknown Deleuze [+ Speculative Realism] (November 2007): 338–339 [307–449].

[26]Sten F. Odenwald, *Patterns in the Void: Why Nothing is Important* (Boulder: Westview Press, 2002), 7.

[27]Oldenwald, *Patterns in the Void*, 109.

[28]Oldenwald, *Patterns in the Void*, 138.

[29]Negarestani, *Cyclonopedia*, 181–182.

on Time and Putrefaction":

> We can say that in decay space is perforated by time: Although time hollows out space, it is space that gives time a twist that abnegates the privilege of time over space and expresses the irrepressible contingencies of the absolute time through material and formal means.[30]

Negarestani's rot-thought likewise sets up an important relation of the interior and the exterior in both ontological and epistemological concerns.

This is not to ignore the spatial dimensions of decay, where "dimensions and metrons deteriorate beneath the machinery of rot"[31] non-metrically, disintegrating objects in a non-fragmentary way.[32] Proceeding in an ostensibly anti-Deleuzian fashion, Negarestani notes: "Chemistry starts from within, but its existence is registered on the surface; ontology is, so to speak, merely a superficial symptom of chemistry."[33] Understanding the acidity of space-time against the soft infirmity of matter is paramount for any realist articulation of geophilosophy. Or as Grant puts it, geology is the corpse grinder of the earth.[34]

Furthermore, in his unpublished essay "Triebkrieg," Negarestani discusses the two traumas of the earth in relation to internality and externality. He writes:

---

[30] Reza Negarestani, "*Memento Tabere*: Reflections on Time and Putrefaction," http://blog.urbanomic.com/cyclon/archives/2009/03/memento_tabi_re.html.

[31] Negarestani, *Cyclonopedia,* 186.

[32] Negarestani, *Cyclonopedia,* 187.

[33] Negarestani, *Cyclonopedia*, 187.

[34] Iain Hamilton Grant, "At the Mountains of Madness: The Demonology of the New Earth and the Politics of Becoming," in *Deleuze and Philosophy: The Difference Engineer*, ed. Keith Ansell Pearson (London: Routledge, 1997), 96.

> If geophilosophy is a philosophy that grasps thought in relation to earth and territory, then it is a philosophy that, perhaps unconsciously, grasps thought in relation to two traumas, one precipitated by the accretion of the earth and the other ensued by the determination of the territory. Whilst the former trauma lies in the consolidation of the earth as a planetary ark for terrestrial life against the cosmic backdrop, the latter is brought about by a combined geographic and demographic determination of a territory against the exteriority of the terrestrial plane and fluxes of populations of all kinds.[35]

It is the former trauma with which this text is concerned. Against Heideggerian and Agambenian fascinations with the open, homeness, and so forth, Negarestani does not subject place or *topos* beneath a phenomenal sensibility or sense of being, but instead notes the tensions between lifeforms (not forms-of-life) and territories—territories as hunks of matter and biological and socio-political demarcations.

If Negarestani's texts pull out the dark spatial ramifycations of a realist geophilosophy, then Martin Hägglund's philosophy can be taken as a temporal addendum to Negarestani's twisted space. Hägglund's highly innovative reading of Derrida's work, elaborated in *Radical Atheism* and subsequent projects, develops a fascinating articulation of time and space's relationship. Hägglund argues that time is ultratranscendental[36] and must be, first and foremost, a logic of succession and not a category of thought that is (phenomenologically) obsessed with the present.[37] Time must be spatialized or thought in terms of the becoming-time of

---

[35]Reza Negarestani, "Triebkrieg" (unpublished manuscript), 5.
[36]Martin Hägglund, *Radical Atheism: Derrida and the Time of Life* (Stanford: Stanford University Press, 2008), 10.
[37]Hägglund, *Radical Atheism*, 15–16.

space,[38] where space is what remains after temporal succession. Hägglund further argues that the time of survival is the very is-ness of life.[39]

The thrust of Hägglund's argument runs against the psychoanalytic bastion of the death drive, for Hägglund suggests that life means survival and not, as Freud suggested, an irrational drive beyond desire which may or may not result in self-destruction. Hägglund's use of time rallies against philosophical uses of immortality. He speaks of Derrida's mortal germ as something "inseparable from the seed of life," writing,

> To think the trace as an ultratranscendental condition is thus to think a constitutive finitude that is absolutely without exception. From within its very constitution life is threatened by death, memory is threatened by forgetting, identity is threatened by alterity, and so on.[40]

Or, following Land's reading of Freud, life itself becomes merely a labyrinthine route toward death.[41]

Time and space are each the trace of the other leaving behind materiality, a materiality which confirms the mortality of both the living and the non-living as well as the increasing difficulty in separating the two, given the violent force of succession. How and if succession can be separated from decay becomes a complex problem.[42] This complexity arises not only from the function of decay but also from the massive knot of epistemology and ontology and their subsequent

---

[38]Hägglund, *Radical Atheism*, 18.

[39]Hägglund, *Radical Atheism*, 33–34.

[40]Hägglund, *Radical Atheism*, 19.

[41]Land, *The Thirst for Annihilation*, 47.

[42]On the relation of succession and anthropocentricity, see Julian Barbour's *The End of Time: The Next Revolution in Physics* (New York: Oxford University Press, 1999).

indistinction. As Land writes,

> This coherence of existent knowing has always been taken by philosophy to be the evident principle of ontology, or the harmonious reciprocity of knowing/being. From Plato, through the Scholastics, to Descartes and beyond, thought presupposes and confirms existence, just as existence bears witness to its origin in divine ideation. . . . Only an immortal entity is able to reflectively apprehend pure being, without becoming inevitably lost in the swamp of matter; that dangerous compacted mass of being and annihilation, malignantly metaphoric, infectious, gnawed, and rotten with time.[43]

This onto-epistemological indistinction is of course only an indistinction from the point of view of thinking beings, whereas the collusion of decay and process is deeply metaphysical. Again, Land is the most useful touchstone here:

> As the destroyer the universe is time, and as the destroyed nature, but in the destruction nature sloughs off the crust in which it had petrified itself and infests time like rot, regressing to its molten core; base matter, becoming, flow, energy, immanence, continuity, flame, desire, death.[44]

As Land reiterates through his text, reason and its material manifestations (civilization, religion, etc.) only serve as a poor salve to this wound. The trauma between process and decay becomes one of the limits of thinking, of the madness of reason.

It is impressive that Negarestani manages to short circuit

---

[43]Land, *The Thirst for Annihilation,* 81.
[44]Land, *The Thirst for Annihilation,* 96.

the madness of reason and thinking of rot-as-process. Rot cannot be seen as merely the undermining of bodies, as only a negative undoing completely separate from the formative processes of nature, as seen above in the quotation from Land.

In his essay "Undercover Softness: An Introduction to the Architecture and Politics of Decay," Negarestani engages medieval theorists of rot to explore the somatically nullifying mathesis of their philosophies. As Negarestani confirms, "the troubling aspect of decay has to do more with its dynamism or gradation than with its inherently defiling nature."[45] He continues:

> Decay does not result in the equivocation between putrid and wholesome; it rather constructs both ideas as its gradationally proper forms, so that what is considered wholesome can in fact be seen as a rotten derivative of an initial construction that has limitropically diminished.[46]

The most interesting thrust of Negarestani's piece is the relation between exteriors and interiors inaugurated by decay: "To put it simply, decay is a process that exteriorizes all interiorities via their own formal or ideal resources."[47] Further, decay builds towards the exterior via the formation of nested interiorities.[48] These interiorities, once taken into thought, are traumas—with trauma here understood as interiorized exteriority. While the psyche attempts to nest (back in the earth) the exterior barrage of nature's succession, in the end (since thought itself is an outgrowth of nature), the nested traumas only open the thinking individual up to

---

[45] Reza Negarestani, "Undercover Softness: An Introduction to the Architecture and Politics of Decay," *COLLAPSE* VI: Geo/Philosophy (January 2010): 382 [379–430].
[46] Negarestani, "Undercover Softness," 383.
[47] Negarestani, "Undercover Softness," 385.
[48] Negarestani, "Undercover Softness," 386.

further ungroundings and regroundings.

These traumas plant instabilities within the earth and initiate the internal ungroundings we will explicate. To engage a complex matrix of ungroundings and groundings means to build, or at least start to articulate, a metaphysics that escapes both the somaphilia of Kant, in which collections of bodies are woven via consciousness, as well as any vitalism (whether classical or modern) in which the substantiality of matter is given too little attention.

Exaggerating decay means both pushing it to the smallest extremes—as perforating particle, the micro-meteorite which punctures the hull, the small projectile of rail gun (fictional and factual), and the thrown-about atomic ammunition of particle accelerators—and also to the largest degree, in the destruction of massive bodies based on machinic and cosmological ruptures.

The first task is to construct, through somewhat strange means, a theory of ungrounding, both internally and externally. A realist theory of ungrounding, following Negarestani, must engage with decay, with the intensive interaction between forces and bodies, without allowing either to abject or exterminate the other.

1.4. WORMS, OR INTERNAL UNGROUNDING

Internal ungroundings function on various scales. The small function of decay of the tiny earthworm (within the carcass or the soft soil) meets the colossal destruction of the worm in the manifestations of speculative literature, films, and videogames. With the Riftworm (from *Gears of War*), the Antlions (*Half Life 2*), the sand-worms of *Dune*, the graboids from *Tremors*, the cytidic Mongolian death worm, Edgar Allen Poe's Conqueror Worm, as well as H.P. Lovecraft's and Thomas Ligotti's various horrific utilizations of worms both large and small, the worm has enjoyed—and continues to enjoy—a

lively speculative life. To get a strong grasp of the oddness of internal ungrounding, it will be helpful to pass through the lairs of the worms.

Poe's Conqueror Worm is the least literal and is generally viewed as a representation of inevitable death, as that which gobbles up masked angels. But still, the worm carries all the weight of death and decay, invoking the giant dragon-like worms of medieval maps.

> Out—out are the lights—out all!
>   And, over each quivering form,
> The curtain, a funeral pall,
>   Comes down with the rush of a storm,
> While the angels, all pallid and wan,
>   Uprising, unveiling, affirm
> That the play is the tragedy, 'Man,'
>   And its hero the Conqueror Worm.[49]

The giant worms of Frank Herbert's *Dune* are the most well-known worms in science fiction. They are enormous creatures that churn the sands of the planet of Arrakis, and are worshipped by its inhabitants (the Freemen) as Shai-Hulud, or "the old man of the desert." The crystalline-toothed gargan-

---

[49]Edgar Allan Poe, "The Conqueror Worm," *Wikisource*: http://en.wikisource.org/wiki/The_Conqueror_Worm. See also *The Complete Works of Edgar Allan Poe: Vol. VII: Poems*, ed. James Albert Harrison (New York: Thomas Y. Crowell, 1902), 87–88.

tuan worms are driven mad by electrical fields and produce a physiology-altering drug known as *melange* as they move through the ground. The Freemen use the worms to traverse the desert planet and harvest their teeth as daggers. The sandworms are hundreds of meters long and appear as a mix between an earthworm and a sea worm. They have a peculiar relation to their planet, in that, as spawn, or sandtrout, the creatures quartered off all water on their world, turning the sphere into a massive desert.

Besides ungrounding the interior of the earth as common worms do, the sandworms of *Dune* unground the surface of the planet by reducing the planet's biomass almost to nothing. The worms participate in the organic/inorganic blur, as well as in the indistinction of madness and reason as a byproduct of their movement, especially in the production of a spice that has drastically mind-altering effects on the humanoids.

The worms of *Dune* have inspired other invertebrate science fiction horrors. In the military science fiction videogame *Gears of War*, for instance, the depths of the planet Sera are rife with various worms. The largest of these is the rift worm, which is worshiped by the game's antagonists, the Locust Horde. The Locust use the rift worm to sink the cities of man as humans have invaded their underground space (the Hollows) in search of Imulsion, a highly sought-after fluid that can be converted into energy. The planet and its worms from *Gears of War* are less interesting than those of *Dune*, but nonetheless hold an ecological lesson: the outer hollows were used as a dumping ground by humans before the Locust Horde made their way to the surface to begin their genocidal campaign.

The other significant fictional giant worms are the graboids of the *Tremors* film franchise and the Mongolian death worm on which they are based. The Mongolian death worm, according to local accounts, resembles a giant cow intestine and is capable of spitting acid and gener-ating

electricity. The graboids of *Tremors*, which are also called sand dragons, are in many ways smaller versions of the worms of *Dune*. In addition to worms as larger, more ecologically complex versions of their real world selves and as agents of death, worms are also engines of a terrestrial weirdness.

Weird fiction, and particularly the work of H.P. Lovecraft, entertains the strangeness of worms. "What the Moon Brings" is filled with brief musing on odd sea worms. Most disturbing are the worm-people found in Lovecraft's "The Festival," but also in Robert Howard's "Worms of the Earth" and Thomas Ligotti's "Last Feast of the Harlequin." In "The Festival," Lovecraft fictionalizes the Danish physician Ole Worm as a translator of the mad Arab Abdul Alhazred's forbidden grimoire, the *Necronomicon*, citing the following unsettling passage:

> "The nethermost caverns," wrote the mad Arab, "are not for the fathoming of eyes that see; for their marvels are strange and terrific. Cursed the ground where dead thoughts live new and oddly bodied, and evil the mind that is held by no head. Wisely did Ibn Schacabao say, that happy is the tomb where no wizard hath lain, and happy the town at night whose wizards are all ashes. For it is of old rumour that the soul of the devil-bought hastes not from his charnel clay, but fats and instructs the very

> worm that gnaws; till out of corruption horrid life springs, and the dull scavengers of earth wax crafty to vex it and swell monstrous to plague it. Great holes secretly are digged where earth's pores ought to suffice, and things have learnt to walk that ought to crawl."[50]

Negarestani situates the above passage as an outline of Lovecraftian poromechanics, which allow for the emergence of the Outside from within the Inside.[51] The earth as a worm-infested body illustrates the structural twist of the operation of nemat-space, in that the void does not merely unground the earth into oblivion. Indeed, such envoiding is necessary for the very possibility of architecture.[52] The best geophysical detail of Lovecraft's "The Festival" is the "oily underground river," which is described as "that putrescent juice of earth's inner horrors."[53]

It is important to note the difference in the use of the worm: for Lovecraft the worm is about the possible and terrifying transmutations of the human, whereas for Negarestani the worm and worming indexes a more disturbing and twisted aspect to nonhuman life-in-itself.[54] Ligotti revisits the strange worm cult in "The Last Feast of the Harlequin," in which an academic becomes one of the worm-like people who gather in the depths of the earth. Ungrounding and sub-humanity are also found in *The Descent*, both Jeff Long's novel and Neil Marshall's unrelated horror film of the same name. Underground human life often leads to demonology. In Long's novel, a race of cannibalistic human-like creatures are

---

[50] H.P. Lovecraft, "The Festival," in *The Fiction: Complete and Unabridged*, ed. S.T. Joshi (New York: Barnes and Noble, 2008), 262–269.
[51] Negarestani, *Cyclonopedia*, 44.
[52] Negarestani, *Cyclonopedia*, 45–47.
[53] Lovecraft, "The Festival," 268.
[54] I owe this point to Nicola Masciandaro.

discovered living under the earth, suggesting the possibility of a historical Satan (which we will explore later).

We can also consider the Shoggoths, the amorphous biological digging machines from Lovecraft's novella *At the Mountains of Madness*, which were engineered by the "Great Old Ones" as slaves (living machines). Lovecraft describes them this way:

> It was a terrible, indescribable thing vaster than any subway train—a shapeless congeries of protoplasmic bubbles, faintly self-luminous, and with myriads of temporary eyes forming and unforming as pustules of greenish light all over the tunnel-filling front that bore down upon us, crushing the frantic penguins and slithering over the glistening floor that it and its kind had swept so evilly free of all litter.[55]

At the Mountains of Madness is a masterpiece of weird fiction that repeatedly invokes notions of deep time as two researchers explore an ancient city built by the Shoggoths for the Great Old Ones. The Great Old Ones existed on the earth aeons before the rise of humanity from the slime pits, and it is suggested that the creation of human life on the earth might be a result of the Great Old Ones' failed experiments in bioengineering. Land explores the possibility of Shoggothic Materialism through the invented figure of Hank Hackhammer. While it is unclear what such a materialism would be, the Shoggoths can easily be tied to the oddness of underground construction and internal ungrounding. Again, from *At the Mountains of Madness*:

---

[55]H.P. Lovecraft, *At the Mountains of Madness*, in *The Fiction: Complete and Unabridged*, ed. S.T. Joshi (New York: Barnes and Noble, 2008), 802.

> For this place could be no ordinary city. It must have formed the primary nucleus and center of some archaic and unbelievable chapter of earth's history whose outward ramifications, recalled only dimly in the most obscure and distorted myths, had vanished utterly amidst the chaos of terrene convulsions long before any human race we know had shambled out of apedom. Here sprawled a Palaeogaean megalopolis compared with which the fabled Atlantis and Lemuria, Commoriom and Uzuldaroum, and Olathoc in the land of Lomar, are recent things of today—not even of yesterday; a megalopolis ranking with such whispered prehuman blasphemies as Valusia, R'lyeh, Ib in the land of Mnar, and the Nameless city of Arabia Deserta.[56]

The apparent massiveness of this megalopolis is elided in the surface of a flat horizon, yet at the same time, it becomes big enough that it can serve as a stage for all living things. The actions of the Shoggoths and their wormy compatriots demonstrates life as an ungrounding force that essentially porositizes the earth—an exaggeration of the lowly earthworm that aerates the soil with its piston-like movement and restructures the soil for better drainage of water. The part of the earth influenced by the activities and biological residue of earthworms is appropriately called the drilosphere.

This Shoggothic, or perhaps vermicular materialism, that we have articulated in the above few pages is intended to emphasize that the organic and inorganic co-conspire to unground, and that it does not take much to realize that one cannot merely slap on peasant shoes and stroll across the open as if the ground beneath one's feet were stable. In addition to the fact that the ground crawls with life both on and beneath

---

[56]Lovecraft, "At the Mountains of Madness," 759.

its thoroughly porositized surface, the matter of the shoes themselves, strange artifice that they are, are always already defamiliarized.

Ligotti's indirect response to Heidegger's "The Origin of the Work of Art" can be seen in the following:

> The most everyday objects may turn peculiar and uncanny if we focus on them long enough, as if they were functionless lumps of matter-questionable and alien. Some old shoes in a clothes closet catch your eye and appear as shapes you have never before pondered. Soon you are not as at ease with them as you once were. . . . You select a pair of shoes to wear and sit down to put them on. It is then you notice your stockinged feet . . . and the body to which they are connected . . . and the universe in which that body is roving about with so many peculiar and uncanny things.[57]

Ligotti ruthlessly opens humans to the exterior, not an exterior that is romantically exteriorized from the human brain itself, but, following Negarestani's rot-thought, one that is coiled up and nestled in the softest parts of our brain. It is for these reasons that Ligotti argues that horror is more real than we are.

It is therefore also horrific that we are capable of creating and utilizing tools that go even further in ungrounding, or even degrounding, that very place (the earth) on which our feet happen to be more or less planted. That is, the human capacity to carve and dig into the earth points to the oddness of how created objects themselves have little solid ground—and yet they are capable of the eradication of the very surface of the earth.

---

[57] Thomas Ligotti, "Introduction," in Stuart Moore, Joe Harris & alia, *The Nightmare Factory* (New York: Fox Atomic Comics, 2008), 84.

2: EXTERNAL UNGROUNDINGS

Design an extraordinary machine which is for killing that which exists so that which does not exist may be complete.
> Louis Aragon, *A Wave of Dreams*

We have gone even further and destroyed the land behind us!
> Nietzsche, *The Gay Science*

2.1. EXTERNALITY AS SPATIAL TORSION

Science fiction frequently utilizes the spatial torsion of the tiny and the large. This is epitomized by the shot early in J.J.

Abrams' *Star Trek* (2009), where the villain Nero's ship the *Narrada* (exiting from a churning singularity) confronts the USS *Kelvin*, with the former's massive bulk reducing the latter to a speck—the difference between a watermelon and a kernel of corn. The divide between the immense and the miniscule simultaneously suggests the ridiculous insignificance of the assault (because of the enemy's pure massiveness), and also the potential explosion of the immense by the unpredictable power of the small (akin to the destructive particle or the viciousness of the microbe). In its perfection, the destructive minuscule approaches a kind of pure perforating monad— that which breaks through the hardest of objects (representing the supposed obdurate purity of the individuated thing)—as the tiny gets closer to the flow of pure space-time. This bears a political dimension, as much of science fiction involves rebellion against an oppressive empire. The opening scenes of both *Star Wars: A New Hope* (1977) and *The Empire Strikes Back* (1980) invoke both the division between the immense and the miniscule as well as differing relations of the empire to the rebellion in terms of spatial torsion. In the first scene of *A New Hope*, a massive sheet of detailed metal passes by to reveal a gaping hole (a docking bay) attempting to swallow the comparatively small rebel ship. That is, the technological massiveness of the empire attempts to overrun the smaller entity. In the second film, in a seemingly more intelligent (or perhaps desperate) act, the same massive ship releases a swarm of probes in order to find the rebels out in the vastness of space. In terms of technique, the ship mimics the shift from direct war to network-centric tactics in the world at large. We will return to network war and the war machine below.

Of course, the striking visuals of the spatial torsion only re-emphasize the unpredictability of a materiality made of powers and flows and not objects, or at least not objects that are anything more than temporary arrests or slowings-down of those powers. But this cannot lead one uncritically to a romanticism, simply repeating the triumphant spirit of utopian science fiction in terms of destabilizing the galactic asymmetry. Joss Whedon's space-western film *Serenity* (2009) plays with this image both politically and in the visual sense, when, once again, the massive fleet (or ship) is met by a far smaller and rebellious force. The ship, the *Serenity*, is soon followed by a mass of its own, not of allied ships but a cloud of vessels controlled by the Reavers—blood-crazed creatures who were the result of a failed experiment performed some years earlier by the alliance, and who are led into battle by a trick of the *Serenity* in a moment appropriately referred to by the captain of *Serenity* as "chickens come home to roost." The visual torsion, then, is short-lived, and the political dimension is complicated, as the triumphant rebel fleet is not rebellious at all but is merely made up of mindless vengeance-seekers functioning only as tools of political change.

Tapping again into Negarestani's rot-thought, we can take Whedon's scene as a lesson against the pure power of the infinitesimal rebellion.[58] It is helpful to quote Negarestani at length here:

> [T]he problem of infinitesimal persistence (becoming infinitely close to zero but never effectively

---

[58]Negarestani, "Undercover Softness," 387.

becoming zero) poses yet another perplexing quandary in regard to the process of decay, a problem which can be summarized as follows: If the decaying object never completely disappears, and, in so far as it continues to become less, generates derivatives and maintains a germinal capacity, then does this mean that death never occurs and the minimally surviving object can never be fully exteriorized? An affirmative answer to this question surely risks advocating a form of vitalism that is ultimately unable to think exteriority. An outright negative answer can also lead to a form of utopian naivety.[59]

Between the tiny rebellious ship and the massive monstrosity of empirical domination, or the unexpected free radical of decay and the pure externalized and unanchored war machine, the terrestrial globe appears as something of a tipping point or pivot between the most extreme magnitudes of science fiction. Negarestani circles such a possibility with his concepts of ( )hole complex and bacterial archeology. The glossary of *Cyclonopedia* defines the terms as follows:

( )hole complex reinvents the Earth as a machine to speed the return of the Old Ones; its convolution irrevocably impairs the repressive Wholeness of the Earth.

Bacterial Archeology. . . . Invigorating the germ-infested chemistry of the Earth by turning it to ( )hole complex; unearthing the planetary sphere as an irreducible complexity of reciprocal links between terrestrial epidemics and cosmic chemis-

---

[59]Negarestani, "Undercover Softness," 387–388.

tries or anonymous materials.[60]

The science fictional always ends up back on the planet, for vessels only function as a temporary ground. Large machinic constructions function as a ground unto themselves as well, in many cases ungrounding the earth, participating in the Earth as ( )hole complex, through the unnatural holing of the earth through excavation. The immense/tiny distinction mentioned above can be represented, in both terrestrial and non-terrestrial realms, in the restless forms of the vortex, whirlpool, maelstrom, etc.

The vortical is rampant in science fiction: black holes, spatio-temporal disturbances, singularities, warp gates, wormholes, etc. These anomalies give space a material constitution, likening it to an environment or ecosystem.

After musing on cyclones, Nick Land writes: "A dark fluidity at the roots of our nature rebels against the security of *terra firma*."[61] Land goes on to note how reason acts as a salve against the fluidity of nature. The chapter where Land has this discussion is entitled "Fanged noumenon," and, as the title implies, Land argues that noumena cannot be an epistemological limit but rather are an ontological fact. In other words, noumena are fanged because they do not remain harmlessly domesticated in the cage of Kantian categorization, but rather, damage and determine us and our thinking by their very nature.

Schelling's philosophy, and in particular the early naturephilosophical stage of his work (Schelling's *Naturphilosophie*), holds the most useful articulation of the vortex in the image of the whirlpool. In the *First Outline of a System of the Philosophy of Nature*, he writes:

The chief problem of the philosophy of Nature is

---

[60]Negarestani, *Cyclonopedia*, 237.
[61]Land, *The Thirst for Annihilation*, 107.

not to explain the active in Nature (for, because it is its first supposition, this is quite conceivable to it), but the resting, permanent. Nature philosophy arrives at this explanation simply by virtue of the presupposition that for Nature the permanent is a limitation of its own activity. So, if this is the case, then impetuous Nature will struggle against every limitation; thereby the points of inhibition of its activity in Nature will attain permanence.[62]

Schelling then illustrates this in a footnote with the image of the whirlpool:

a stream flows in a straight line forward as long as it encounters no resistance. Where there is resistance—a whirlpool forms. Every original product of nature is such a whirlpool, every organism. The whirlpool is not something immobilized, it is rather something constantly transforming—but reproduced anew at each moment. Thus no product in nature is fixed, but is introduced at each instant through the force of nature entire.[63]

The tension that Schelling encircles is that of identity and process. The problem is: how is the whirlpool, or any product of nature, identified as such a product, given the tumultuous status of all objects? As Schelling emphasizes, "The product is originally nothing but a mere point, a mere limit, and it is only though Nature's battling against this point that it is, so to speak, raised to a full sphere, a product."[64]

The most impressive and violent of whirlpools is the

---

[62] F.W.J. Schelling, *First Outline of a System of the Philosophy of Nature*, trans. Keith R. Peterson (Albany: State University of New York Press, 2004), 17–18.
[63] Schelling, *First Outline of a System*, 18.
[64] Schelling, *First Outline of a System*, 205–206.

maelstrom, an extreme whirlpool which appears in Jules Verne's *20,000 Leagues Under the Sea*, Edgar Allan Poe's "A Descent into the Maelstrom," and briefly in Herman Melville's *Moby-Dick*. The mention in *Moby-Dick* is brief and is only to emphasize Ahab's willingness to pursue the white whale to the ends of the earth, as the maelstrom mentioned is the Moskstraumen off the coast of Norway. Both Verne and Poe erroneously tie the maelstrom to the depths of the sea, when in fact it is a surface event created by cross-streams.

Charybdis, the monster of Greek myth who spat out whirlpools and often appeared as a whirlpool, not only appears as an indeterminate object but as the edge of a disastrous object, as the space between Charybdis and Scylla (another watery monster), a space between two disasters, a space that is dominated by a lack of energy. The tension between the immense and the miniscule in the science fictive, mentioned above, resonates with the energetic poles of Charybdis and Scylla. Between the vortexes, vortexes that in themselves are objects with a minimal boundary, we have an expansion downwards and upwards, as well as side-to-side. This torrential spatiality is further complicated by the fact that whirlpools and vortexes are themselves conflicting forces in a particular medium, raising the question of the materiality of the whirlpool or the vortex.

The figure of the whirlpool explores what externality means in a material sense. Simply put, the vortex, the whirlpool, becomes the manifestation of the very process of externalizing on the surface, indexing the very concept of depths, both terrestrially and otherwise. That is, it shows the weirdness of spatial expansion within a particular medium. The question becomes one of the expansive movement of the whirlpool, whether the vortex expands at the top (towards immensity as a kind of grounding, in the Schellingian sense) or digs downwards towards its point, thereby ungrounding (towards the intense internality of the terminus). In order to explore the exaggerated yet minimalist materiality of the vortex, we will double this exaggeration through odd, hyperbolic examples: digging machines and planet demolishers.

2.2. DIGGING MACHINES

The digging machine is a fundamentally cartoonish image, a completely unfeasible project. It is that which inhabits the vortical space—as opening the ground behind it, and forming a new ground in front of it as it digs. Most real digging machinery (particularly that used for mining) remains on the surface of the earth, destroying layers of surface with machinations, explosives, and chemicals, while sub-surface mining utilizes techniques of mazing already discussed in 1.3 above (via the concept of Negarestani's architectural decay). Surface machinery (such as that used with strip mining) often comprises fundamentally ridiculous constructions—certain excavators are among the largest land vehicles on Earth. The massiveness of these machines speaks to the bizarre extremes required to forge the digging machines that exist in speculative fiction. The digging machine is taken to a ridiculous extreme in the film *The Core* (2003). Negarestani aptly describes the film thus:

> The movie begins with scenes of a tellurian cataclysm: an electroconvulsive sky, disoriented animals, scrambled communication signals and agitated birds. The earth's core has stopped spinning, and consequently the dynamism of all flows and convection currents at the core have been brought to an abrupt halt. . . . The movie depicts the last human attempts to reactivate the core and prevent the Earth from becoming one with the Sun.[65]

---

[65] Negarestani, *Cyclonopedia*, 161–162.

The film's protagonists, with endless funding from the US government, set about to bore into the earth in order to strategically place nuclear warheads at the core to recharge it—making the antagonist the Earth itself. The scientists construct a snake-like vehicle called the *Virgil*, powered by the fictional Unobtanium, and using lasers to carve through the Earth's strata. The team encounters various problems, the first two relating to the unexpected hardness of the earth itself: a cavern of geodes and a pocket of diamonds. The team has to sacrifice segments of the *Virgil* in order to augment the nuclear explosions. One of the team members discovers that the slowing of the core was caused by the US government using an experimental weapon that causes tactically useful earthquakes. Oddly, the film thus shows the merging of the Earth and the Sun as caused by a regrounding of the earth and stopped by the re-Sunning of the Earth—igniting its core.

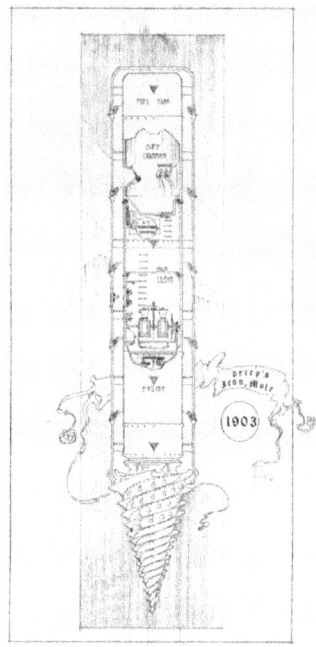

Excavations that start from the surface are fairly common in fiction. Edgar Rice Burrough's *Pellucidar* novels come to mind, and in particular *At the Core of the Earth*, which contains a drilling machine called the iron mole and the subterranean prospector. The series of novels explores the hollow Earth, as the iron mole takes the novel's characters below the surface of the Earth to the interior's surface. The world of *Pellucidar* is, like many regions in hollow Earth novels, a prehistoric one, where the vanquished species of the

Earth have migrated. Several novels involving terrestrial journeys reground the Earth's interior, as the earth below us is made to be familiar, just like the surface we know. Verne's *Journey to the Center of the Earth* is particularly disappointing in this regard, as the explorers find a fungal forest and a small ocean.

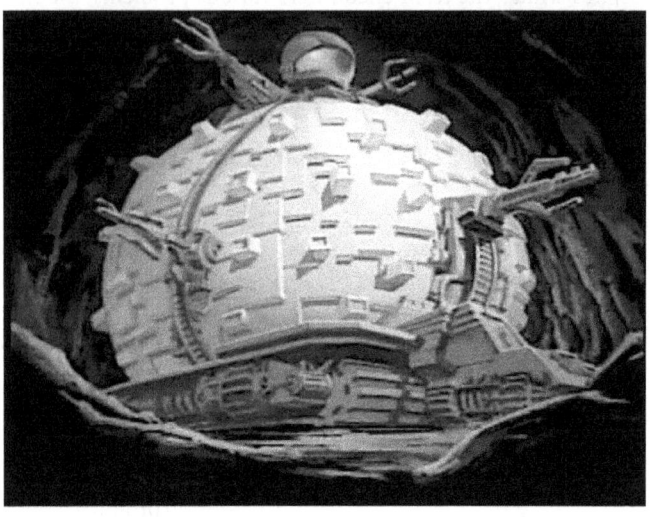

The *Technodrome* of the *Teenage Mutant Ninja Turtles* cartoons and videogames is, like Nero's *Narrada*, a redoubled ungrounder. Not only does it dig beneath the earth, it also harbors a transdimensional portal. It is also one of the most bizarre digging machines, as it is doubles as a weapon of mass destruction. The *Technodrome*, with its arsenal of weapons and especially its transdimensional portal, is always situated in the best place to create collisions between the dark and volcanic dimension X with our world.

The *Technodrome*, like the *Narrada*, redoubles ungrounding as both terrestrial digging and opening of portals that disregard spatial limitations. Subterranean digging machines, unlike the surface destroyers of the mining industry, not only unground and rework the earth, but also occupy the space that they dig out. The minimal safe distance of the excavators is completely lost in the work of the digging machine as the device carves its own open, blasting the contours of its own horizon.

External ungroundings not only unground, but also resurface and re-horizon the terrestrial space around them. The very concept of surface becomes nothing more substantial than the recent activity upon it. As Manuel De Landa writes,

> In terms of the nonlinear dynamics of our planet, the thin rocky crust on which we live and which we call our land and home is perhaps the earth's least important component. The crust is, indeed, a mere hardening with the greater system of underground lava flows which, organizing themselves into large 'conveyor belts' (convective cells), are the main factor in the genesis of the most salient and apparently durable structures of the crusty surface.[66]

This of course does not mean that humans are bound to exist on an open surface but can, and have, existed (at least to some degree) beneath the earth. Perhaps Zarathustra desired an escape underground as he himself lamented the surface of the earth: "The earth has a skin; and this skin has diseases and one of them is man."[67] He states that the sublime man's happiness should "smell of the earth and not of contempt for the earth."[68] Perhaps Zarathustra should have returned to his cave once the earth became too round for him.[69]

For humans living in subterranean cities, digging machines would function as a device of ecological and archi-

---

[66] De Landa, *A Thousand Years*, 257–258.
[67] Friedrich Nietzsche, *Thus Spoke Zarathustra*, trans. R.J. Hollingdale (London: Penguin Books, 2003), 153.
[68] Nietzsche, *Thus Spoke Zarathustra*, 140.
[69] Nietzsche, *Thus Spoke Zarathustra*, 284.

tectural expansion and less like a destructive entity. The function of machines in such a space is already required by the massive metropolises of the modern world: "[T]he toroidal world of self-intersecting drains and sewers built beneath developed cities all over the world . . . gives shape to the dominant mantra of modern architecture, that form follows function, with an intensity, and a necessity, that surface structures seldom achieve."[70] Furthermore, underground cities, such as those in Cappadocia, Turkey, will long outlast those on the planet's storming surface.[71]

To borrow from Deleuze and Guattari, a body (or assemblage of diggers in this case) can make itself into a war machine that interacts with the other nebulae of machines here—the other machinic assemblage being the stratified earth[72]—going about territorializing and deterritorializing the earth. Drug smugglers make themselves into a digging machine to circumvent US borders just as Bin Laden's followers maze their way into the mountains to avoid detection.[73]

The fear of detection via ungrounding takes an extreme turn in the *Matrix* film trilogy. In the second and third *Matrix* films (*The Matrix Reloaded* and *The Matrix Revolutions*, both released in 2003), ungrounding is reversed, as it is humans who are usually the agents of ungrounding, moving towards the unknown of the earth. In the films, however, the antagonistic robotic life-forms, which control the earth's surface, dig their way towards Zion (the last human city) while the humans huddle close to their geothermal heat, armed to the teeth. As the tentacled sentinels dig deeper and deeper, the humans unground themselves defensively, moving closer and closer to the heat engine of the Earth's center.

---

[70] Geoff Manaugh, *The BLDGBLOG Book* (San Francisco: Chronicle Books, 2009), 53.
[71] Manaugh, *The BLDGBLOG Book*, 79.
[72] Deleuze and Guattari, *A Thousand Plateaus*, 353.
[73] Manaugh, *The BLDGBLOG Book*, 84–85.

The ungrounding machines of the sentinels meet the ungrounding machine of the last humans of Zion, both of which are not concerned with surfaces but only with destroying each other, regardless of the charred earth between them. The possibility of a totalizing unleashing of machines, which is the cause of all the troubles in the *Matrix* series, brings us to the total planetary destruction of planet killers.

2.3. PLANET DEMOLISHING

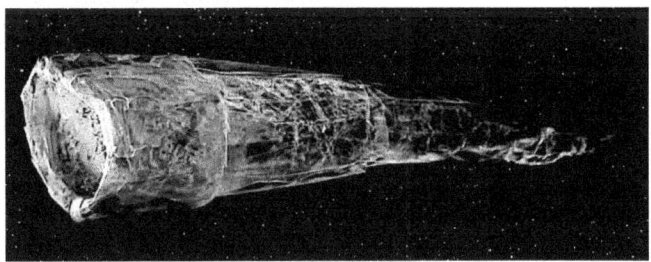

To go even further in terms of external ungrounding and grounding, it is necessary to leave the earth's surface entirely. Taking the ungrounding movement of the digging machines off the surface of the planet, the vortical, the whirlpool, and the storm become entities in themselves. Such manifestations occur in science fiction.

The most well-known planet killer is no doubt *Star Wars*' *Death Star*. The *Death Star* uses a powerful laser to obliterate planets that dare to defy the empire. The *Death Star*, through impossible energy expenditure, smooths out space since it is a war machine that replaces what it destroys, a sphere of complete militarization, though its weaknesses are quickly exploited and the machine is destroyed. Far more impressive planet killers exist in science fiction.

The creature featured in the *Star Trek: The Original Series* episode, "The Doomsday Machine," is the most literal actualization of the vortical, as it compacts planets and consumes the result—with its immensity at one end and its terminus at the other. This final point reconstitutes the consumed mass as a monad, a new perforating particle. The energetic funnel entity indexes the most central horror of actual space, that of a black hole.

The black hole as a destructive singularity, as a center of gravity pushing the very fabric of space, is detached from its ultra-weight in the fantasy of planet destroying. Just as terrestrial digging machines worm their way through terrestrial bodies, deterritorialized digging machines (i.e., planet destroyers) move through space and expand the yawning spatiality of space itself.

Internal ungrounding functions in terms of a metaphysical darkening, whereas external ungrounding functions in terms of metaphysical blackening. These different modes can be likened to the cosmosis of decay articulated in Negarestani's "Corpse Bride," where he writes, "the intensive and extensive vectors of decay are imagined as a shriveling body from which a cosmic range of either beings emerge."[74] As a solid strike against somaticism, Negarestani suggests that for anything to remain, given the violent forces of decay, it must always remain less. As he puts it, "intensive diminution is reinforced by extensive subtraction."[75]

Different from worming, from darkening the interior which perforates and restructures the object, the planet killer blackens, removing the entire object to make space (in the cosmological bionome—the cosmonome, or, the capacity for the cosmos to bear life). The consuming vortex creates an even larger possibility for immensity in its clearing of the field as it spreads the very bounds of the field itself towards the boundless.

---

[74] Reza Negarestani, "The Corpse Bride: Thinking with *Nigredo*," *COLLAPSE* IV: Concept Horror (May 2008): 143 [129–161].
[75] Negarestani, "The Corpse Bride," 144.

Planet demolishing is an ungrounding apart from a ground, whereas worming regrounds. Worming is a kind of horizontal ungrounding, whereas planet demolishing will unground the grounds, knock the very floor out from under it in a vertical way. Worming appears to be undoing what is beneath, what is under our feet. Worms dig, whereas the doomsday machines and planet killers obliterate horizontally. Planet killing, while apparently horizontal, is ontologically vertical, whereas worming is ontologically horizontal. This is contrary to the ungrounder's actual movement, as worming horizontally opens up the stratification side to side, where digging machines and planet killers (as deterritorialized digging machines) devastate all chance of stratification, except for the complete replacement of a planet by its destroyer.

Negarestani writes that, "Warmachines need an abundant amount of metal to fuel their terminal multiplicity and their tactical anomalies. No metallic entity other than the Earth's core can boast such riches for feeding warmachines with polygentic metals, electromagnetic anomalies (cyber warmachines) and radical schizophrenia."[76] The planet killer as a deterritorialization of the war machine becomes perfected in the villain of Unicron from the *Transformers* (1986) animated film. Unicron is a techno-organic planet-sized entity which consumes other planets to propagate its existence. In this sense, Unicron, as the penultimate planet destroyer, is the perfect war machine as pure exteriority.[77] While Deleuze and Guattari argue through the mouth of Clausewitz that the war machine is only ever improperly conducted by the State, Unicron is an entity the size of the largest entity known as even possibly governable.[78]

As Manabrata Guha shows in his essay "Introduction to SIMADology," the Clausewitzian paradigm of war is thought to be immune to even the strangest war machines, whether tiny or massive. But Guha argues that such thinking does not adequately grasp the complexity of battle space.[79] Likewise, we attack—and will continue to attack—traditional geophilosophy on the grounds that it believes it can contain indefinite worming (which can be likened to small explosions of havoc, which Guha names Singularly Intensive Mobile Agency of Decay) and remain resistant to the Clausewitzian fantasy of absolute war. Whereas Clausewitz's and the geophilosopher's notion of an absolute is limited here, we suggest an absoluteness beyond the very bounds of the terrestrial—the possibility of total planetary annihilation.[80] As Guha puts it, even the Deleuzo-Guattarian war machine fails to grasp SIMAD as the earth is softened and slime-ified by its hypercamouflaged discord.[81]

---

[76] Negarestani, *Cyclonopedia*, 162.

[77] Deleuze and Guattari, *A Thousand Plateaus*, 354.

[78] Deleuze and Guattari, *A Thousand Plateaus*, 355.

[79] Manabrata Guha, "Introduction to SIMADology: *Polemos* in the 21st Century," *COLLAPSE* VI: Geo/Philosophy (January 2010): 342 [323–378].

[80] Guha, "Introduction to SIMADology," 326.

[81] Guha, "Introduction to SIMADology," 328.

2.4. A BRIEF NOTE ON DIRECTIONALITY

It is important to not forget, however, that the very spatiality of up, down, left, and right, and even internal and external, bears an anthropocentric ghost. As Buckminster Fuller argued, when we go up and down we are actually going in and out in relation to the Earth. That is, "up" and "down" ignore the *bending* of gravity. Furthermore, the concepts of sunset and sunrise invoke a flat earth, where in reality, the terms should be replaced by sunclipse and sunsight, as the experience of the earth as phenomenologically flat does not override the earth as a sphere. While folk terms have a certain utility, the theoretical and philosophical weight they bring with them needs to be interrogated.

Any sense of directionality we invoke is always in relation to the Earth or one of its energetic components. Compasses utilize pieces of the Earth to help us follow fixed directions, directions which are aligned with the Earth's magnetic field, yet these field lines are not themselves completely stable. If directionality was a movement on or in relation to only the surface, then movement upwards (away from the planet) would not require the massive amounts of energy that it does. The same can be said of exploring the ocean depths, as moving beneath so much raw matter requires special preparation for humans to survive, suggesting the impossibility of any ground under the water to finally rest on. One could also take the framing of the central narrative disaster in James Cameron's *The Abyss* (1989) as a reminder of this fact. In the film, the underwater station falls deeper underwater, re-ungrounding the experience of the terrestrial and emphasizing that the fall is towards the center of the earth and not any particular direction as we might want to perceive it. Human feet do not determine the reference point for all directionality.

To shift back to another science fictional register, the gigantic worm writhing through tellurian space unlocks all concepts of horizontality. The immensity of the worm appears as a surface effect, but when it disappears beneath the surface, the vortex shifts from the horizontal of space (<) to the vertical of the terrestrial (V). Caves, tunnels, and surface mines expand the horizontal ungrounding to its limit, as the spherical nature of the Earth is simultaneously ignored and tested through the sideways expansion of boring, worming, and so forth.

Vertical ungrounding is that which moves through the surface (through the ground), as both an internal circling and softening of the earth towards collapse (worming), and also as an external bombardment or piercing of the tellurian (as in the planet-destroying machine). Whereas horizontal ungrounding relies on a pre-established surface or ground in order to engage its destructive machinations, vertical ungroundings—those of the vortex—threaten to undo the ground beyond its deepest terrestrial bound.

Nero's enemy ship the *Narrada* (in Abrams' *Star Trek*), discussed above, is of particular interest because it combines both types of ungrounding. It drills deep into the core of the Earth while injecting a special type of matter to begin forming a black hole in the planet's center, thereby consuming it from the inside. The ungrounding is not only simultaneously internal and external, but it creates a vortex that in itself is the minimalist representation of an object, the most basic interruption of the process of being, as already demonstrated in Schelling's whirlpool. If being is process, and the appearance of being is an arrest of that material flow, then it becomes difficult to separate grounding from ungrounding without the ground of either the subject or nature-independent thought. As Iain Hamilton Grant explains,

> If . . . ground is always and irrevocably particular, then natural history can investigate the grounding of ground, but, again in virtue of the nature of the subject of nature, 'nothing original ever appears

itself'. In brief, the transcendental phenomenon has
a physical ground, but physical ground is a product
of the dynamic ungrounding that precedes it as the
subject of nature itself.[82]

Grant explains, contra Deleuze, that ungrounding forces lead to grounds or groundings in a realist sense—that is, a sense outside of our thinking. Instead of the transcendental escaping the physical or overriding it in a Kantian sense, the transcendental is an effect of the deeper power of nature, as the transcendental can never stand alone but only in relation to some thing, as Schelling argues in *The Grounding of Positive Philosophy*.[83]

What then is the fundamental difference between the darkening of the internal ungrounding of worming and the blackening of the external ungrounding of planet demolishing? Darkening functions as a hole-making, an absencing of the solidity of the interior, whereas blackening has a more fundamental ontological acidity, as it tries to make more space out of space. The useful ramifications of both internal and external ungrounding will be explored in the conclusion.

The central concern, the bone passing through both fleshes of these odd machines, is that of time.

---

[82]Grant, *Philosophies of Nature,* 204.
[83]F.W.J. Schelling, *The Grounding of Positive Philosophy*, trans. Bruce Matthews (Albany: State University of New York Press, 2007), 208.

3: REGROUNDINGS

Let's not forget that buildings sit on the Earth.
>> Lebbeus Woods

The Earth is a farm. We are someone else's property.
>> Charles Fort

3.1. XENOARCHAEOLOGY

The errant signals, distress calls, and anomalous readings of science fiction lead to the Cthuluoid ethical encounter of an unavoidable encounter with the weird.[84] One codification of the weird is in the trope of the found text, which redoubles the shocking foundness of the weird. Other codifications of the weird come in spatial and temporal forms. We can see the temporally weird at work in tropes of the mythic and ancient, or of the futuristic penetrating the past (*Stargate*'s alien Egyptians). We can see the spatially weird at work in common science fiction tropes, such as distant planets, dimensional rifts, wormholes, and so on. Both the temporally and spatially weird unground, ground, and reground in fantastical ways.

---

[84]For Negarestani, Cthuloid ethics is an ethics of radical openness, that of 'what is next?' Such an ethics is open to radical butchering, an openness far more dangerous than Levinas' ethics, which amounts to an ethics of affordance and not openness.

The fabric of time and space, assumed to be absolute, comes into question in the aforementioned foundness of the text, and the text (*as* a text) echoes the torsion of time itself in time— that is, the tangible movement of time as synchronic time. It is for these reasons that, in exemplary sci-fi horror (such as the *Alien* series, *Event Horizon*, *The Thing*), something has already happened and the current action is trying to discover what happened or whether what happened is going to happen again.

Alien and weird objects show all objects to be spatially disturbing in a literal horizontal fashion: things simply get in the way as that which we must move through or around. But there is also a vertical depth to objects soaked in allure and fascination, by which we are caught. This is the question of substance, which we will work to complicate, beginning with Bruno Latour's black boxes, Graham Harman's commentary on Latour, and Harman's own elaborations of objects (where objects become non-relational as such). The replacement of substance with black boxes raises the problem of networking, as Harman's critique shows, because they harness a deeper structure. That is, for Harman, it is not only an object's place in a network that matters, because an object contains a depth that cannot be accounted for in purely relational terms.

Harman's *Prince of Networks: Bruno Latour and Metaphysics* provides an extensive review of Latour's corpus before providing a critique of what Harman sees as Latour's reduction of the object in Actor Network Theory (ANT). This critique focuses on the fact that, for Harman, an object is not merely revealed in its actions, connections or networks,[85] but has a vacuum-sealed core that is irreducible, that persists without relations. Harman's object oriented ontology, following a critical elaboration of Heidegger's tool-analysis, asserts that objects consistently withdraw from us. As Harman

---

[85] Graham Harman, *Prince of Networks: Bruno Latour and Metaphysics*, (Melbourne: re.press, 2009), 131.

explains,

> Contrary to the most typical reading of Heidegger, the tool-being of objects cannot be its unconscious usefulness for humans in opposition to its conscious visibility. . . . Any sort of human relation to objects will inevitably fail to grasp them as they are.[86]

The weirdness of objects (and their ontological and epistemological accessibility) is further complicated by time and time is made manifest in the earth that buries the object, obfuscating the history—as well as the capacity—of the object's relationality.

The xeno-archaeological or exo-archaeological assists in wasting or withering the anthropocentricity of worlds (against Kant and Badiou) in a twofold sense. The foundness of the big dumb object (the Clarke-Kubrick Monolith, *Doom 3*'s soul cube, *Dead Space*'s Marker) demonstrates the existence of non-human intelligence and being, as well as the possible end of civilization. These objects are dumb in the sense of being hyper-fetishistically presented as excessive in their object-hood. Nick Bostrom's essay, "Where are They? Why I Hope the Search for Extraterrestrial Life Finds Nothing," explores the anxiety of whether the end to life is early on in life's development or much later (whether through a civilization's self-destruction, a cosmological event that destroys life in its germinal state, or something else entirely). Bostrom's point is that one should hope that the search for life finds nothing, because this would suggest that the development of life, if it ceased, happens early on, and if it were terminated by a much later event, this would mean bad news for the human species,

---

[86]Graham Harman, *Guerrilla Metaphysics: Phenomenology and the Carpentry of Things* (Chicago: Open Court, 2005), 74.

as we may be hurtling toward our inevitable self-destruction.[87]

Big dumb objects could suggest that civilizations are few and far between, possibly leading to exaggerated attempts at communicating, marking, or reaching out towards other civilizations and intelligences. Or, big dumb objects could be the metastasization of the technological excess of auto-apocalyptic ends. The final question is whether extelligence (Jack Cohen and Ian Stewart's term for intelligence that can export itself in the form of records[88]) is particularly rare, or if species with the capacity for extelligence simply tend to exterminate themselves.

Objects become inherently weird, or perhaps, in Negarestani's terms, they become the thing without genesis (i.e., the sacred).[89] The alien object/strange artifact generates mystery (if it generates anything at all), whether it is known to be ancient or disputed, often due to its impossible construction or infinitely long history. A search for the missing object, or an attempt to reconstruct the object, is often implied (the *Lord of the Rings* trilogy is an odd reversal: instead of a search to find and harness the powers of the object, there is a long trek to destroy the object, to take it apart, thereby returning it to the very fire of its creation—a process of devolution). With the odd or long temporality, there is also an ambiguous location or manual ("They are digging in the wrong place," such as in *Indiana Jones and the Last Crusade,* or, "There is always a manual," such as in Luc Besson's *The Fifth Element).* Manual misreading often leads to death (holy grail, ark of the covenant, amulets, etc.) or the repetition of the horror that has already taken place, as is the case with some sci-fi horror

---

[87]Nick Bostrom, "Why I Hope the Search for Extraterrestrial Life Finds Nothing," *COLLAPSE* V: The Copernican Imperative (February 2009): 333–348.

[88]Ian Stewart and Jack Cohen, *Figments of Reality: The Evolution of the Curious Mind* (New York: Cambridge University Press, 1997).

[89]Negarestani, *Cyclonopedia,* 244.

films.[90]

In this narrative structure, the weapon must always be destroyed, forgotten, or rendered inoperable, but with the possibility that it may re-emerge to 'fall into the wrong hands' again. Hence the temporality is ancient—always retracted but always reappearing in any possible present, which necessitates orders, brotherhoods, cults, etc. to protect it, to keep watch (*The Ninth Gate*, the fellowship of the ring, the monks in *The Fifth Element*, knights of the holy grail). These orders must readily copy this odd temporality to protect humanity at large.

Spatially, then, the odd object can pop up anywhere, yet only a few move towards it, and only a few recognize it or know what the object is. The oddness of an alien artifact's spatiality is its disrespect for space—constantly rupturing, bending or otherwise contorting or piercing space itself.

The purportedly ageless or ancient quality allows it to simultaneously disrespect time—time and space being obviously tethered.

3.2. STRANGE TEMPORALITIES

Quentin Meillassoux, in his small but watershed text *After Finitude: An Essay on the Necessity of Contingency*, rallies against postmodern discourses that would bind knowing to reality as perceived by human subjects, thereby locking the world into human parameters—a problematic system of knowledge that Meillassoux names correlationism. Meillassoux writes: "Correlationism consists in disqualifying the claim that it is possible to consider the realms of subjectivity and objectivity independently of one another."[91]

---

[90]It could be argued that, aside from John Carpenter's *The Thing* (1982), all sci-fi horror films fail, as they inevitably transform into another form of horror (by introducing a human enemy) or become another kind of sci-fi (by ending on a classic utopian note).
[91]Quentin Meillassoux, *After Finitude: An Essay on the Necessity of*

As an affront to correlationism, Meillassoux proposes arche-fossils: objects which "[indicate] the existence of an ancestral reality or event; one that is anterior to terrestrial life."[92]

Meillassoux argues that these objects (which are also statements) damage any assertion that would claim the ontological priority of human thought in the universe. Meillassoux systematically addresses the possible correlationist rejoinders, beginning with the fact that the primary response would be that the literal or realist meaning of the statement is overridden by its givenness or the fact that anything must be always already for us.[93] This is the trick of philosophy: accepting the real as unthinkable.[94]

While Ray Brassier seems to support a theory of objects in themselves in his text *Nihil Unbound*—that is, that certain things pre-exist our experience—he is critical of Meillassoux's arche-fossil because it maintains the distinction between anthropocentric time and cosmological time, which allows phenomenologists to disregard pre-experiential time as not existing properly until it is grasped by thought, and therefore Meillassoux's ancestral realm is a reservoir "waiting" to be intuited. The common thread here is that the mythical view of man, the view that any experience prior to the emergence of humanity only has value as it is researched or dug up through our experience, allows for a narrative which is contingent only to serve the centrality of human experience. It is for this reason that correlationist philosophy, philosophy that pays particular heed to Heidegger, is damaging to philosophy proper.

While we have invoked and continue to harness Bruno Latour's concept of the black box, Latour's concept of temporality, which is articulated largely in *The Pasteurization*

Contingency (London: Continuum, 2008), 5.
[92] Meillassoux, *After Finitude*, 10.
[93] Meillassoux, *After Finitude*, 14.
[94] Meillassoux, *After Finitude*, 27.

of France,[95] causes a great deal of worry. Because objects, for Latour, are best understood when they are in action, and in relation with other objects, he states that ferments did not exist prior to Pasteur's discovery of them since they had no visible relations.[96] Latour is not saying that the ferments have no reality, but that, since other relations must ultimately define them and what they can do, they would exist in an entirely different way.[97] Still, Latour, like Meillassoux, seems to suggest two temporalities, perhaps something inherited from Deleuze (as Aion and Chronos). As part of our combat against such temporal divisions, we will engage grounding and ungrounding from the buried object.

The depth of the black box, in the alien object, is sealed from inquiry and analysis, yet it nevertheless perforates the exterior with its seemingly endlessly inaccessible interiority. Substance (as black matter, yet also errantly networked) becomes the interplay of interiority and exteriority, which is slowed down in our perception, in order to grasp or see it:

Interior---->(<^>)--->Exterior

Substance becomes an axis of immensity/minisculity, moving towards the interior and the exterior. An odd object, then, is to be found where these movements are even less discernible than they are in everyday objects.

Not that objects are all readily discernible in their coordinates, but the odd object is unhinged even in its spatio-temporality, which is usually traceable in most objects. We try to discern the interior of the odd object to replicate it, but its pushing outwards, its rupturing of time and space, re-doubles its withdrawnness.

As Negarestani says of the relic, it is that which binds

---

[95] Bruno Latour, *The Pasteurization of France*, trans. Alan Sheridan and John Law (Cambridge: Harvard University Press, 1988).
[96] Harman, *Prince of Networks*, 83.
[97] Harman, *Prince of Networks*, 83.

phenomenologies to temporalities: "a relic is an operative of exhumation which confounds the chronological time by connecting Now with abyssal time scales."[98] Relics, and the exhumations which bring them forth from the terrestrial depths, disturb the purportedly flat (both temporally and spatially) surface of the earth. Negarestani explains:

> Exhumation undermines the order of strata. . . . Exhumation is the invocation of the ground's potencies before they are actualized. . . . Since ungrounding or exhumation incapacitates the consolidating power of ground, the earth cannot be narrated by its outer surface any longer but only by its plot holes, vermicular traces of exhumation.[99]

The nature of the connection between the abyssal and the now deserves some scrutiny if we are to avoid the temporal pitfalls of both Latour and Meillassoux. This connection is not a bridge across difference, across two ontological regimes of time, but across two experiences of measuring them that are often taken to be ontologically distinct: deep time and quotidian time.

3.3. INTERNAL AND EXTERNAL POTENTIALITIES

Negarestani's own analysis or schizo-archive of odd objects and alien artifacts is connected to exhumation, particularly in the case of those labeled as inorganic demons.[100] Negarestani speaks of their aloneness, their status as contagion vectors, and as forsaken things. Often in horror, fantasy, and science fiction, the relics are weapons either complete or broken in

---

[98]Negarestani, *Cyclonopedia*, 242.
[99]Negarestani, *Cyclonopedia*, 239.
[100]Negarestani, *Cyclonopedia*, 223.

reconstructable parts.[101]

Whether weapon or otherwise, the relic or alien object functions as either an "internalizing" or an "externalizing" object; either by pulling energy, objects, flows, etc., inwards (as part of some transformative act) or by exposing others to its energy, influence, etc. We could take the mysterious monolith from Kubrick's (as well as Arthur C. Clarke's) *2001: A Space Odyssey* as a prime example.

The effect of the monolithic computers ranges from advancing primate evolution to causing a kind of super-insanity/super-consciousness in the protagonist. These monolithic computers are vectors of viruses of ideation constructed by the oldest species of the galaxy, the firstborn. They are virtually indestructible automatons which can teleport, self-replicate, open a gate that allows for faster than light travel, and may have dimensions beyond normal perception. They

---

[101] Negarestani, *Cyclonopedia*, 232–234.

are constructed to be impenetrable objects that manipulate the environment around them. The firstborn wanted monoliths to promote, developmentally, the advancement of intelligent species across the universe. This problem assumes, going back to Nick Bostrom's essay, that intelligent life must self-destruct often, unless the end of life appears earlier on.

The monoliths are objects that not only connect the now to abyssal time scales, but were also designed to address the disjunction between lived time and a realist sense of deep time, or, more precisely, future time. The firstborn designed the monoliths to continue their experiments far beyond their own existence.

In many ways, the puzzle boxes of the *Hellraiser* films function as the opposite of the monoliths, as they are a kind of pleasure object or inward-turning object. The boxes, which are also known as Lemarchand's boxes, come in various configurations, the most popular being the Lament Configuration. The boxes function as gateways to another dimension, one where pain and pleasure become indistinguishable at the hands of the Cenobites, demon-like entities that manipulate the flesh of human beings.

The puzzle must be rearranged and solved in order to open a schism between the world of humans and that of the cenobites. The puzzle box of *Hellraiser* is intensely alluring, yet it explodes the darkness of its own interiority outwards once the human has solved its riddle. The allure of the box, along with the soft musical tones it emanates, works to draw in the solver so that he completes the puzzle, unlocking its darkness. The puzzleboxes—unlike the monoliths—are disgustingly selfish, and time is completely disregarded in the weird space of their torture and allure.

Allure, following Harman, is "the separation of an object from its qualities,"[102] the sensual "notes" that stream forth from an object and become objects in their own right.

---

[102] Harman, *Guerrilla Metaphysics,* 153.

Furthermore, allure pushes the real object to a distance, rearranging "our comportment so that we now occupy ourselves directly with notes that were previously enslaved to some other object of our attention."[103]

When we engage the puzzle box, we forget its smooth blackness (or its gold ornamentation in the film version) as our fascination makes the object a kind of thing in itself, although rearranged by our perception of its sensual "notes," its "allure" (only superficially re-arranged, it might be added). While Harman argues that allure can happen between non-human actors (as they also "strike" against each other's sensual facades), the problematic issue is whether the language of human fascination can be properly divorced from Harman's anti-correlationist, post-phenomenological approach to the object.

Jane Bennett's *Vibrant Matter* attempts to change passive objects into animate things through an engagement with Latour, Deleuze, Spinoza, and others, arguing that a certain vitalism could help us to reorient ourselves to the agency and tendencies of inanimate objects. Bennett begins her book by an account of a material fascination. She writes:

> Glove, pollen, rat, cap, stick. As I encountered these items, they shimmered back and forth between debris and thing—between, on the one hand, stuff to ignore, except insofar as it betokened human activity (the workman's efforts, the litterer's toss, the rat-poisoner's success), and, on the other hand, stuff that commanded attention in its own right, as existents in excess of their association with human meanings, habits, or projects.[104]

---

[103]Harman, *Guerrilla Metaphysics,* 180.
[104]Jane Bennett, *Vibrant Matter: A Political Ecology of Things* (Durham: Duke University Press, 2010), 4.

While this quotation from Bennett describes the power of things, it also overwhlems them with human affect, or human fascination. Like Bennett and Harman, Timothy Morton, in *The Ecological Thought,* attempts to articulate a similar materiality that cuts across (or encompasses) the organic and the inorganic, calling this concept the mesh.[105] Morton writes:

> The ecological thought stirs because the mesh appears in our social, psychic, and scientific domains. Since everything is interconnected, there is no definite background and therefore no definite foreground. Darwin sensed the mesh while pondering the implications of natural selection.[106]

Morton goes on to discuss the mesh in terms more relevant for geophilosophy:

> The ecological crisis makes us aware of how interdependent everything is. This has resulted in a creepy sensation that there is literally no world anymore. We're losing the very ground under our feet. In philosophical language, we're not just losing 'ontological' levels of meaningfulness. We're losing the 'ontic,' the actual physical level we trusted for so long.[107]

Setting aside Morton's division of the ontic and the ontological in terms of meaningfulness, his mesh attempts (similar to Bennett and Harman) to give to the inorganic its own vitalism and "life," but this mesh may have, nevertheless, too many roots in human brains—and is thereby worthy of suspicion.

---

[105] Timothy Morton, *The Ecological Thought* (Cambridge: Harvard University Press, 2010), 28.
[106] Morton, *Ecological Thought*, 28.
[107] Morton, *Ecological Thought*, 31.

Part of my suspicion arises from the lack of a discussion of the temporal dimension in Harman, Bennett, and Morton. At the end of *The Ecological Thought* Morton discusses the conundrum of hyperobjects—objects that exceed the capture and temporalities of the human race (such as plutonium, global warming, etc.). Morton does not elaborate on the relations between objects, temporality, and allure. The alien artifact and the act of exhumation both engage these three themes simultaneously, yet the radical theories of objects and of the vibrant (and supposedly non-correlationist) materiality of things cannot really account for a temporal allure—that is, the possibility of a non-human fascination with objects within inhuman and post-human time scales.[108]

The difficulty will hinge upon considering relics as tools for a new geophilosophy—and not merely as objects that would index past human cultures, the traces of which happen to be encased in a useless earth. Because Latour's objects are so connected across various actions that they reverse time, and Harman's objects are so vacuum-sealed that time seems to manipulate only an object's surface effects, Latour and Harman thereby evade the problem of genesis.

Instead of focusing on allure and fascination, one might attempt to explain objects as part of a generative nature, and not merely one that is meshed, withdrawn, or vital.

3.4. THE ORGANIC/INORGANIC BLUR

Bennett, in further arguing that things have a force of

---

[108] Morton does however approach the subject of how objects "time" and "space" in his more recent book *Realist Magic* (Ann Arbor: Open Humanities Press, 2013). And Harman also addresses some space-time considerations, in relation to objects, in several of his works; see, for example, Graham Harman, "Time, Space, Essence, and Eidos: A New Theory of Causation," *Cosmos and History: The Journal of Natural and Social Philosophy* 6.1 (2010): 1–17.

themselves, argues that humans, as things, have a kind of power—but that we need to readjust our sense of time to see this power.[109]

Bennett talks specifically about the process of mineralization. After engaging the work of Manuel De Landa, Bennett writes:

> In the long and slow time of evolution, then, mineral material appears as the mover and shaker, the active power, and the human beings, with their much-lauded capacity for self-directed action, appear as its product.[110]

Bennett does not return to the problematic nature of fascination, however, nor does she consider how thought and life are forms and terms that might need serious revision.[111]

Going back to Hägglund's articulation of the trace as well as Meillassoux's arche-fossil, we can see that the relic, the alien artifact, and so forth, all suggest patterns not only of past life but of the cycle of extinction for all life (or perhaps of all recognizable activity, regardless of its organic or inorganic status).

We would like very much to be able to wipe someone or something off the face of the earth, but such an action is beyond our capabilities. The constant reminder of the relic speaks not only to the stubbornness of objects but also to the trace structure that they invoke—that life comes from and leaves behind traces that, while seemingly completely separate from life (in terms of an organic/inorganic distinction), in fact complicate any attempt to ontologically quarantine life in

---

[109] Bennett, *Vibrant Matter*, 10–11.

[110] Bennett, *Vibrant Matter*, 11.

[111] Bennett has, however, previously addressed an entire book to the subject of fascination and its relation to ethics; see Jane Bennett, *The Enchantment of Modern Life: Attachments, Crossings, and Ethics* (Princeton: Princeton University Press, 2001).

order to privilege it from non-life. This cocooning allows for further qualifications of life as it is injected either with pure immanence (Michel Henry), joy (Deleuze), will or power (Nietzsche, Schopenhauer, etc.), and so forth.

As Ligotti puts it wonderfully in "The Sect of the Idiot," "Life is a nightmare that leaves its mark upon you in order to prove that it is, in fact, real."[112] Videogames, strangely enough,

---

[112] Thomas Ligotti, "The Sect of the Idiot," in *Songs of a Dead Dreamer* (Burton: Subterranean Press, 2010), 238. One of Ligotti's main inspirations is Arthur Schopenhauer, whom he engages at length in his remarkable text, *The Conspiracy Against the Human Race*. Schopenhauer is of particular use, as his pessimism—being far more radical than Nietzsche's—allows for a truly contingent and decaying nature. One particular danger of such extreme pessimism, as Wolfgang Schirmacher shows, is that,

> The human being, according to Schopenhauer, is of all suffering creatures the only one that through insight can break the cycle of eat-and-be-eaten and thus become a paragon for all creation. The voluntary extinguishing of the will to life in ourselves would allow humaneness to triumph over nature. What at first appeared as resignation would then reveal itself to be a successful way out.
>
> But can something that looks like collective suicide by the human species be called successful? Today, anthropofugal impulses are stronger than ever, and it doesn't take a prophet to predict our species' suicide within the next millennium. A humanity that simply continues as usual with its theory and practice, its conflict management and ideology of progress, is doomed. Admitting to ourselves that the conflicts are unresolvable, that with the theoretical and practical means we have at our disposal we are merely attempting to treat the symptoms: such an admission could well amount to a turning point. But lobbyists, whether they receive their mandate from the state, the economy, culture, or religion, reject any notion of admitting to their own bankruptcy. They see self-criticism merely as a strategy for entrenching their own influence.

have the most bizarre articulations of strange forms of life. The game *Deadspace*, in particular, has a fascinating form of life with strange geophysical horrors.

In the game, a massive space ship goes to a planet in order to crack it, to remove a giant piece of the planet's crust for mining purposes. Before beginning the operation, the crew discovers a marker, a large stone object covered in markings believed to be a holy relic by a paranoiac Scientology-like religion. Humans in the vicinity of the marker become enraged and begin killing one another on the planet's colony, and soon it becomes obvious something is amiss.

A microorganism, a particularly nasty creature of awful bio-spatial plasticity, begins to mutate humans into grotesque monsters multiplying and misaligning their body parts. The marker, as a container of mutagenic life, indexes the emergence of life from non-life, thereby hammering home the contingency and pure materiality of the category of life. While

---

See Wolfgang Schirmacher, "Technoculture and Life Technique," in *Just Living: Philosophy in Artificial Life* (New York: Atropos Press, forthcoming), 3.

Bennett addresses the possibility of non-organic life, she relies on Deleuze's concept of life as immanent.[113] As already discussed in 1.1 above, Deleuze's concept of immanence relies on nature as pre-thinkable, thereby undercutting nature's creative and destructive vitality.

To return to Bennett's exploration of mineralization, we see that living things, and in particular entities such as humans, thought to be separate (whether theologically or technologically) from the engine of nature, are in fact themselves stratified by processes. The capacity of a brain to think cannot be ontologically different from the process of mineralization; the difference must be grasped in terms of the interiorizing and exteriorizing potentialities of the ontic layering of the world.

As a final note, the odd life of vital materialism and regrounding can be found in Bryan Singer's *Superman Returns* (2006). In the film, Superman's arch-nemesis Lex Luthor goes to the Fortress of Solitude (Superman's miniature crystal island, located in the arctic) and steals a piece of crystal technology that originated on Superman's home planet Krypton. Luthor then breaks into a museum and acquires a meteorite fragment of Krypton, binding the materials together before launching them into the ocean. The weaponized crystal-mineral quickly grows into a new continent that, due to water displacement, will drown most of the United States and coastal regions around the world.

Luthor creates the one commodity that is always in demand: new earth. Furthermore, Luthor binds kryptonite to the crystal in order to protect it from Superman, thereby pre-radiating a new landmass to keep Superman at bay. In order to destroy Luthor's material act of regrounding, Superman literally ungrounds the entire continent by burrowing beneath it, ripping the crystal out of the ground, and tossing it into the sun. We can see this as indexing Negarestani's conflict of the

---

[113]Bennett, *Vibrant Matter*, 54–55.

earth's insider with the sun. The weaponization of the earth, as we explore geocontainment in the next section, speaks to the vitalism of the inorganic, in that it is both as generative as organic life and more temporally stable than the organic.

Instead of appreciating the longevity of the organic, as well as its instability (i.e., it is not merely a ground to walk upon), approaches characterized by what I will call geocontainment demonstrate that the earth and the process of stratification become a massive grave to bear, hold, and conceal, especially in accordance with phenomenology and humanistic concerns.

3.5. GEOCONTAINMENT, OR THE PANIC OF BURIAL

In addition to the relics, the exhumed, and cataclysmic mineralization, there are also the geotechnics of hyper-futuristic technology and the oddness of the assumption that anything stays buried. This is true of both the animate and inanimate. Eastern and Western modes of burial differ significantly in their articulation of the "homeness" of the dead, employing vastly different forms of thanato-stratification. As Kristen Alvanson argues in "Elysian Space in the Middle East," the dead in the Middle East are buried on top of one another with flat stones atop of them so that passers-by can walk on them and across the markings of the dead. Alvanson writes,

> The site of the graveyard bridges the ontological contents of the living and the post-mortem pro-trusion of these contents, thus marking the transition from ontology to theatrical ontology.[114]

---

[114] Kristen Alvanson, "Elysian Space in the Middle East," *COLLAPSE* II: Speculative Realism (March 2007): 257 [257–271].

Put otherwise, the graveyard binds the affect of ontology to ontology at an obscenely intimate level. Furthermore, Alvanson argues that Islamic graveyards disrupt regular thinking since, following Heidegger, dwelling is bound to thinking and Islamic graveyards flatten all capacity for dwelling.[115] It becomes impossible to stand apart from the dead, and one is always standing on top of them. This bearing of the dead is, from the Western point of view, too close for comfort, as the earth is supposed to separate the dead from the processes of mourning that occur "above ground."

The necrological and the geocentric are subsequently joined, regenerating the ideological split of the ecocentric and anthropocentric. The Earth is reterritorialized to function as the final home for bodies supposedly both hidden and protected. Ashes to ashes, dust to dust: this kind of thinking ontologically deadens the earth in order to cement the theological or otherwise supra-anthropocentric divide between the body and the spirit.

How far back the religiosity of burial goes is a contested issue. The burial of the dead goes back at least as far as *Homo sapiens* communities dating to hundreds of thousands of years ago. There is, of course, no way to know whether burial occurred because of social, spiritual, or merely practical reasons. But the earth as ultra-grave is not only for the burial of expired organic life, but is also sought out for the containment of dangerous chemicals and radiation.

In the Nevada desert lies Yucca Mountain, formed millions of years ago by ashen explosions from cauldron-like volcanoes composed of pyroclastic rock. Its thermal characteristics make the location an excellent candidate for the disposal of radioactive waste, and over the last twenty years the mountain has been molded for just this purpose through massive portals dug into the rock. Large alcoves were hollowed with explosives to make room for scientific

---

[115] Alvanson, "Elysian Space," 266.

experiments.

Millions of dry casks filled with heavy metals were to be transported via truck and rail. As of the present moment, the repository's opening is to be scaled back and perhaps eliminated all together. Deep geological repositories are modeled after naturally occurring fission reactors, such as in Oklo, Africa, where the local groundwater is protected by layers of sandstone and granite. Oklo shows that the central problematic is not the containment capacity of the repository, but the questionable stabilities that arise once the waste needs to be moved to the site. Much of the concern over Yucca Mountain has been construed in terms of terrorist fantasies revolving around the possible theft of materials to construct dirty bombs as they are transported by train. Our concern here, however, is not the potential logistical and political disasters that could result from such transportation, but the geo-mechanical implications of the support for these deep repositories and the possible responses to them.

Sites such as Yucca Mountain imply the possibility of an absolute solution for the burial of the problematic waste of modern life. That is, Yucca Mountain is posited as a permanent burial site meant to contain what is never to be moved again. Its out-of-sightness, seemingly in support of the Husserlian dictum that "the earth does not move," seems more than slightly dismissive of the future of the earth and the capacity of human stewardship (although, human life may not have much longevity). Even the very practical operation of waste management demonstrates the inflexibility of anthropocentric thought's determination of life over nature, a life that is not the possibility of organicity, but is rather a phenomenologized form of life in the Kantian sense. Furthermore, the earth is codified as a ground, but a dead ground—a platform for human activity from which ideation somehow manages to escape.

Another repository's fixity has taken on an almost demonological appearance: at the Waste Isolation Pilot Plant in Loving, New Mexico, designed to house transuranic radioactive waste for 10,000 years, an interdisciplinary collaboration is attempting to design a massive temple of warning to any living being that would approach the site, communicating its message in a slew of languages and pictographs to ward off any future investigator. One proposal suggests the construction of fearsome looking spikes to convey danger and harm.[116]

But one can imagine, as similar things have occurred in various science fiction works, that a fearsome looking temple would only facilitate attraction and allure—an elaborate construction, regardless of its fearsomeness, would invite investigation.

Even more radical than the Waste Isolation Pilot Plant is the Russian Hot Drop Project, which argues that spent nuclear material should be deposited in the depths of the earth. Instead of digging a deep well, the project's scientists argued that the waste cold be placed in a ball of tungsten and heated up to 1,200 degrees Celsius so that it well melt its way down to a safe distance.

Such elaborate constructions and measures only further suggest the oddness of a purportedly permanent solution in a purportedly dead earth. The assumption of an already dead Earth is clearly apparent in the fact that waste is to be placed between the water table and the surface. It is not that a system can be made that will not fail, but that the Earth is represented as having an inert character it does not have simply for peace of mind. The neglect of the Earth's dynamism is coupled with the strange desire for waste to remain unseen.

The purported permanence of Yucca Mountain invokes another strange philosophic dimension, not in terms strictly relevant to the earth and its reduction to a body, but in an odd

---

[116]For examples, see smudge studio, "Containing Uncertainty: Design for Infinite Quarantine," *Friends of the Pleistocene* [weblog], February 24, 2010: http://fopnews.wordpress.com/2010/02/24/containing-un certainity-design-for-infinite-quarantine/.

temporality. The buried wastes are a byproduct of contemporary practices that threaten the physical continuity of human existence.

This threat is ignored, most likely due to the anthropocentric delusion that the transcendental ego will somehow outlive biological death. Or, to put it another way, the infinite time of burial at Yucca Mountain functions to house human waste in order to guarantee the endless time of human thought.

The ecological burial of the wasted present to save the abstract vitality of human consciousness denies the power of matter and earth to propagate new forms of life, quarantining the parallel putrefaction of our actual being as well as the truths of putrefaction, necrosis, and (radioactive) decay, all stirred in an anthropically corrupted temporality.

The real meaning of terrestrial burial and of earthly temporality, following Jan Zalasiewicz, is simply that the earth will ultimately bury us and every single trace of our existence. On long enough time scales, all relics and artifacts will be demolished. As Zalasiewicz writes in *The Earth After Us*,

> The surface of the earth is no place to preserve deep history. The surface of the future Earth, one hundred million years from now, will not have preserved evidence of contemporary human activity. One can be quite categorical about this. Whatever arrangement of oceans and continents, or whatever stat of cool or warmth will exist then, the Earth's surface will have been wiped clean of human traces.[117]

To return to the nuclear, it is, of course, not merely a byproduct of power generation, but also a naturally occurring

---

[117] Jan Zalasiewicz, *The Earth After Us: What Legacy Will Humans Leave in the Rocks?* (New York: Oxford University Press, 2008), 14.

phenomenon in radioactive isotopes. The natural advent of radioactive isotopes has allowed for the weaponization of the earth itself, moving us back to the demonic and the infernal.

In *The BLDGBLOG Book*, author Geoff Manaugh suggests that a passage in Milton's *Paradise Lost* anticipates (in some mix of literality and metaphor) the discovery of an earthy superweapon, possibly uranium: a stone with massively explosive potential. Manaugh quotes the following from *Paradise Lost* in service of Milton the Atomist:

> These in their dark nativity the Deep, Shall yield us, pregnant with infernal flame, Which, into hollow engines long and round Thick-rammed, at the other bore with touch of fire.[118]

Besides the obvious examples of weaponization and the apocalyptic capacities of the nuclear, plutonium has been used, in mostly abortive attempts, to redesign the earth both above and below the surface. In the late 1950s and early 1960s, at Livermore Radiation Laboratory in California, scientists theorized that nuclear weapons could be used to create harbors and canals.[119] The Plowshare program proposed even using nuclear bombs to create more direct train routes in the southwest United States.[120] As Tom Zoellner notes in *Uranium*, the Plowshare program began with Project Gnome,[121] in which a nuclear device was going to be detonated under the ground to boil water in the aquifer in order to generate power from the steam. Despite the initial tests' complete failure, over two dozen more warheads were detonated.

Even more ridiculous combinations of massive weapons

---

[118]Manaugh, *The BLDGBLOG Book*, 245.
[119]Tom Zoellner, *Uranium: War, Energy, and the Rock that Shaped the World* (New York: Viking Press, 2009), 101.
[120]Zoellner, *Uranium* 101.
[121]Zoellner, *Uranium* 102.

and geophysics are possible. Manaugh suggests a possible future with terrestrial weaponization resulting from the accidents of experiments. Manaugh writes: "In late 2006, Swiss engineers found to their surprise that they had set off a series of small tremors in the city of Basel when they began injecting water into a freshly drilled geothermal well on the outskirts of the town."[122] Even stranger, Manaugh continues, "Taipei 101, one of the tallest (and heaviest) buildings on earth, might actually have reopened a dormant fault beneath the island nation of Taiwan."[123] There is not much more to say than Zalasiewicz does about the chaos of the surface of the Earth: "Our planet is too active, its surface too energetic, too abrasive, too corrosive."[124]

To close, we must burrow deeper into the earth, into the strange potentiality of infernal geologies.

---

[122] Manaugh, *The BLDGBLOG Book*, 240.
[123] Manaugh, *The BLDGBLOG Book*, 240.
[124] Zalasiewicz, *The Earth After Us*, 15.

4: HELL DIMENSIONS

> The world is deep: and deeper than day has ever comprehended.
> Nietzsche, *Thus Spoke Zarathustra*

4.1. HELL IN (>), OR INFERNOLOGY AS GEOPHILOSOPHY

Geoff Manaugh suggests the possibility of a topography of hell:

> Could we assemble a catalog of landscape metaphors and geographical analogies writers have used over the centuries to describe this hellish underworld? It's not hard to imagine some obscure papal academy in Rome publishing tract after tract on the exact geotechnical nature of the Inferno.[125]

Hell is an all too familiar landscape, often a volcanic region with roaming demons or floating rivers of souls more or less terrestrial. The first most simple distinction to make is that between the chthonic underworld and the non-spatialized otherworld.[126] For our geophilosophical purposes here it is the

---

[125] Manaugh, *The BLDGBLOG Book*, 88.
[126] Alice K. Turner, *The History of Hell* (New York: Mariner Books, 1995), 5.

former that concerns us. Hell, in its chthonic configuration, suggests an odd short circuit between the earth as a shallow phenomenological playground and a deeper understanding of the earth as a complex geological system. This very distinction is blurred by the interchangeability in German transcendental philosophy of reason and ground, or between *Vernunft* and *Grund*.[127]

But before engaging the philosophical dimension, a tour of the plane, or perhaps, the colony of hells is necessary. There are a plethora of spatial hells: *Sheol* (the pit or grave), *Gehenna* (the valley just outside of Jerusalem), *Hades* (as the grave), and *Infernus* (what lies underneath). Negarestani discusses the place of the abomination beyond the dung gate thereby situating hell as landfill in the following manner:

> Near the city of Jerusalem, behind the Dung Gate (Nehemiah 2:13), in the valley of Hinnom, Tophet or the Place of Abomination was located. The Dung Gate (an architectural climax for urban-waste), as described in the book of Nehemiah, was at the southernmost tip of Jerusalem, near the Pool of Siloam. It was a main exist to the Valley of Hinnom (*ge hinnom*), where the city disposed of its garbage. The valley is a deep, narrow ravine running through Jerusalem. . . . The origin of the name Hinnom is not clear, but is usually said to derive from a 'son of Hinnom' (*ge bhen hinnom*) who apparently owned or had some significant associations with the valley at a time prior to Joshua. It is the Hebrew name Hinnom that later transforms into the biblical and Koranic words for Hell.[128]

---

[127]Salomon Maimon, *Essay on Transcendental Philosophy* (London: Continuum, 2010), 61.
[128]Negarestani, *Cyclonopedia*, 155.

In addition to these historical places, several popular hell mouths have been nominated. The Masaya volcano in Nicaragua, the cavern entrance to Mayan hell in Belize, St. Patrick's Purgatory in Ireland, the underground river entrance to Hades at the southern tip of Greece, the Hekla volcano in Iceland, and, most impressive, the Erta Ale volcano in Africa. The overwhelming volcanic nature of the hell mouths will be discussed below. First the geographic possibilities of hell must be, at least, partially exhausted.

Despite the numerous maps of hell within Dante's *Inferno*, the geologically and geographic descriptions of hell are not as prevalent as one would think. There is the lower city of hell[129] (*Dis*) and the stench-filled abyss,[130] steep slopes above rivers of boiling blood,[131] and so forth. The most particular geological features of Dante's hell are that of the *malebolgia*, or literally, "evil pockets."[132] The pockets are a series of ten valleys filled with the worst sinners of lower hell tormented by their demonic slave masters. The *malebolgia* are another example of redoubled ungrounding, or hell inside hell. The very concept of a pocketed hell indexes hell as an impossible geo-spatial "hold" of misery.

Hell becomes a strange fascination of another geological space, of the strange distance of geology as it invades non-theological geological endeavors.

4.2. VOLCANIC ORIFICES

In 1970 in the USSR, a scientific adventure began deep into the depths of the Earth. Digging past 40,000 feet, the Kola Superdeep Borehole found interesting results. The hole, which

---

[129] Dante, *The Divine Comedy, Volume I: Inferno*, trans. Mark Musa (London: Penguin Books, 1984), 147.
[130] Dante, *Inferno*, 168.
[131] Dante, *Inferno*, 176–177.
[132] Dante, *Inferno*, 231.

despite its depth only went through a third of the Earth's crust, encountered strange entities such as rocks filled with water and mud boiling with hydrogen gas. An urban legend quickly arose.

On the History Channel's *Gates of Hell* television show, a story no doubt related to the borehole project was recounted. A bishop and a paranormal investigator who host a radio show played an audio recording supposedly captured by seismologists who accidentally recorded the screaming of the damned when they lowered microphones into the earth. The literality of hell rests on the aforementioned split between the chthonic and the otherworld, between immanence and transcendence.

The split between the otherworldly and the chthonic parallels the split between *Vernunft* and *Grund*, or between the transcendental and the immanent. Yet this relation of transcendence and immanence is not Kantian or Hegelian but Schellingian, and is bound up with the volcanic. The volcanic acts a pivot between both hell/earth and transcendence/immanence. As we've seen, hell mouths are frequently volcanic, and the volcanic has a particular philosophical history as well. For example, in Nietzsche:

> There is an island in the sea—not far from the Blissful Islands of Zarathustra—upon which a volcano continually smokes; the people, and especially the old women among the people, say that it is placed like a block of stone before the gate of the underworld, but that the narrow downward path which leads to this gate of the underworld passes through the volcano itself.[133]

The philosophical assessment of the volcanic is caught in the gravity of Empedocles' apocryphal leap into the fiery breach of

---

[133] Nietzsche, *Thus Spoke Zarathustra,* 152.

Mount Etna. To this we can add Novalis' poetic explorations of the salt mines where he toiled; Lucretius and Aristotle's theorizations of wind friction deep in the Earth; Plato's rivers of heat; the earth gorging itself on vapor, mountain oil, and sulfur, subsequently releasing gas, or, for Johannes Kepler, tears and excrement. James Hutton, the father of modern geology, conceives of the Earth as a great heat engine, thereby marking the shift into a slightly more scientific consideration of the terra-depths as infiltrated by actuating powers.[134]

No philosophical articulation of volcanism can match Athansius Kircher's. Kircher, a 17th-century polymath, devoted an entire work, *Mundus Subterraneus*, to the study of volcanoes, concluding that the fiery constructs comprised a kind of inverted astronomy. This term was popularized by Siegfried Zielinski, who borrowed it from Novalis' *Heinrich von Ofterdingen*, in which the figure of the hermit states that, while the astronomer sees the future in the stars, the investigator of the deep past understands the primeval history of the earth.[135]

This dark or underground astronomy was further solidified by Hölderin's portrayal of the aforementioned death of Empedocles; by tying the worldly thinker to the mythological figure of Icarus, he thereby linked the distant sun to the bubbling lava of Etna.

It is here that we can directly engage the volcanic transcendental geology of Schelling's naturephilosophy (*Naturphilosophie*). In Schelling's post-Kantian naturephilosophy, the earth is both the unground of the transcendental (in nature's capacity to produce thought) and the biological graveyard of history (the fact that life itself is subject to the flux of nature). This stands in opposition to the already discussed somaticism of Kant.

---

[134]Siegfried Zielinksi, *Deep Time of the Media: Toward an Archeology of Seeing and Hearing by Technical Means* (New York: MIT Press, 2006), 21–22.

[135]Zielinski, *Deep Time of the Media*, 41.

4.3. AGAINST OVER-DEMONIZATION

In other words, for Schelling, the generative nature of the earth becomes the very being of transcendence. However, this transcendent being is only a being to the extent that it is also a productivity. As Grant succinctly puts it:

> The dilemma initially facing a transcendental naturalism is accordingly that it must either assert determination by contingent entities of whatever nature (things, forces) or assert parochialism and admit that even in those of its theses that putatively address nature, no such address takes place insofar as the 'nature' in question is phenomenal only.[136]

The endless ungrounding of Schelling's naturephilosophy cannot and should not be equated with the sort of infinite potentiality found in a Deleuzian virtuality, which remains structurally ideal.

The specter of anthropocentric thinking, which hides best in Deleuzian virtuality, appears as the shadow that demonizes hell, and which transforms the geophysical capacities of hell into ones of perverse minds. In other words, infernology is often overridden by demonology,[137] whether the demons are materialized creatures of hell itself or merely demons of the mind.[138] This is why there are far more demons in *Difference and Repetition* than geophysical transcendences.

---

[136] Iain Hamilton Grant, "Prospects for Post-Copernican Dogmatism: The Antinomies of Transcendental Naturalism," *COLLAPSE* V: The Copernican Imperative (February 2009): 421 [415–451].

[137] Turner, *The History of Hell*, 4.

[138] See Sigmund Freud, *Totem and Taboo* (1913), in *The Standard Edition of the Complete Psychological Works of Sigmund Freud*, ed. and trans. James Strachey, Vol. 13 (London: Hogarth Press, 1955), 1–161, and Christian Kerslake, "Deleuze and Demons," in *Deleuze and the Unconscious* (London: Continuum, 2007).

This fall into demonology is an unfortunate part of Jeff Long's *The Descent*, where explanations of the reality of the sub-earth are dropped in exchange for a realization of demons or *Homo hadalis*. The upshot of this is at least twofold: first, Long's *Homo hadalis* suggests a deeper connection between the innards of the earth and the evolution of human beings, and second, it realizes, on a more metaphysical scale, that the possibility of being itself is rooted in the darkness of the earth.[139]

In temporal terms, hell seems to have a timeless dimension, yet time continually penetrates it in order to deposit the dead, and then recedes again. Hell is atemporal to the degree that time passes through it without harm. Furthermore, the fact that Hell can be entered and exited (the first being much easier) reinforces the ways in which hell's time can be expanded and contracted. Various tales of entering hell speak to the tortures of hell lengthening time. Hell-time is drastically out of joint. From this strange space-time, it is hell's exports that we seek to glimpse next.

4.4. HELL OUT (<)

> Maybe our world is another planet's hell.
> Aldous Huxley

> She tore a hole in our universe.
> *Event Horizon*

Paul W.S. Anderson's science fiction horror film *Event Horizon* is the best experiment in the unkempt spatiality of hell. In the film, the ship the *Event Horizon* disappears for several

---

[139]Nicola Masciandaro, ed., *Hideous Gnosis: Black Metal Theory Symposium I* (New York: CreateSpace, 2010), 112.

years and is presumed lost only to reappear in orbit of Neptune sending out a distress signal to earth. Another ship, the *Lewis and Clarke*, is sent to investigate the strange message which is composed of screaming and mumbled Latin words, such as, *liberate tuteme ex inferis* ["save yourself from hell"].

En route, the ship's designer Doctor William Weir explains that the ship employed an experimental gravity drive capable of generating a portal between two points in space, enabling it to travel faster than light. After boarding the ship and encountering odd horrors, the rescue team soon realizes that the ship was in hell, a realm of pure chaos, and that the *Event Horizon* came back as a living entity, driving the crew members to madness, causing them to rape and mutilate one another, and that this is what has started to happen to the crew of the *Lewis and Clark*.

This maddening chaos has a distinctly Meillassouxian source. For Meillassoux, the absolute, that which stands as the foundation for the possibility of knowledge, is chaos and nothing but. As Meillassoux writes, "Our absolute, in effect, is nothing other than an extreme form of chaos, a hyper-Chaos, for which nothing is or would seem to be impossible, not even the unthinkable."[140]

In his essay "Subtraction and Contraction," Meillassoux connects themes of chaos to death. Following a Bergsonian line of thinking, Meillassoux argues that instead of death being a return to the inorganic, death would be a form of madness:

> If matter is what Bergson says it is, then death . . . would not at all be identified with nothing, but rather with madness—and even an *infinite madness*. . . . To make an image of death, we would have to conceive what our life would be if all the movements of the earth, all the noises of the earth, all the smells, the tastes, all the light—of the earth and elsewhere, came to us in a moment, in an instant—like an atrocious screaming tumult of things.[141]

Event Horizon is interesting simply because hell becomes one spatial dimension among many, ripping it from its usual chthonic location and giving it its own existence altogether— an existence which is either the becoming-material of madness or the madness of becoming-material.

Furthermore, to return to the odd object and alien artifact, the work of artifacts perpetuate the mythical/ demonological where hell becomes another spatial dimension. The alien artifact withers anthropocentricity via the objective quality of the object (such as in the opening pages of Žižek's *Parallax View*). In the weird story, the artifact is hyperbolic in its object status is also over-present (withdrawn and too close). As we have seen in 3.1 above, the alien artifact is withdrawn from a concept of world, but the hellish artifact

---

[140]Meillassoux, *After Finitude*, 64.
[141]Quentin Meillassoux, "Subtraction and Contraction: Deleuze, Immanence, and Matter and Memory," *COLLAPSE* III: Unknown Deleuze [+ Speculative Realism] (November 2007): 104 [63–107].

goes even farther and brings chaos.

Whereas the madness of the *Event Horizon* is contained within the ship, the insanity of hell from other sources, such as that of the *Doom* videogame series, is not confined to one locale, but seeps out and spills across whole dimensions.

In the videogame *Doom 3*, which is set in 2145, the United Aerospace Corporation, the largest corporation in existence, has constructed a large research facility on Mars' moon Phobos. As an unnamed marine, you are sent to investigate the disappearance of a scientist involved with the company's teleportation experiments. An accident occurs and the forces of hell begin to invade the base. While science fiction and sci-fi horror have made extensive use of trans-dimensional portals, *Doom 3* does the best job of articulating the connection of a non-chthonic or hyper-chaotic extra-dimensional hell to the possibility of technological jumps between dimensions.

As the game progresses, you (as the marine) learn that an archaeological dig on the surface discovered an odd artifact called the soul cube, a device built by an ancient civilization as a defense against hell. The cube functions as a miniature weaponized hell—gathering souls until it becomes charged. By moving off-world, the game is able to maintain the strange indexing of the alien artifact as well as the possibility of an other-worldly hell becoming a chthonic one as the demons attempt to open a portal to earth.

The futuro-techno portalization of the hell-gate retroactively engenders the seep of hell into other technological manifestations, most notably in war, with the phrase "war is hell," and the possibility that things go or went to hell while also remaining on Earth's surface.

We can approach this form of insanity via Nick Land's "Meat," with his ramblings on *Heart of Darkness*: "Arriving reprocessed from inexistence at phase transition into hell, or the future. . . . Pandemonium scrolls out in silence."[142] This cryptic remark finds roots in *The Thirst for Annihilation* in the following: "the world of work perishes with the One, and that zero is the engine of war."[143] Hellish war is, first and foremost, a war that does not serve the state,[144] and, following Bataille, "War is the free movement of solar flow across the earth."[145]

Jake and Dinos Chapman's sculpture *Fucking Hell* (2008) further drives the techno-futurism of hell seepage in an underhanded way.[146] *Fucking Hell* is a rather large swastika-shaped diorama which portrays the horror of the holocaust to an almost comically exaggerated degree. The scene is filled with body parts, speared heads, crucified victims, cybernetic Nazi soldiers, emaciated corpses, death camp fences, over-

---

[142] Nick Land, "Meat (or How to Kill Oedipus in Cyberspace)," *Body and Society* 1.3-4 (1995): 191–204.
[143] Land, *The Thirst for Annihilation*, 147.
[144] Land, *The Thirst for Annihilation*, 148.
[145] Land, *The Thirst for Annihilation*, 149.
[146] Jake & Dinos Chapman, *Fucking Hell* (2008), exhibited at White Cube, London, 2008: http://whitecube.com/exhibitions/jake_dinos_chapman_if_hitler_had_been_a_hippy_how_happy_would_we_be_masons_yard_2008/.

stuffed boats and trains, etc. The Chapmans' piece invokes b-movie nasties of the 1980s as well as, perhaps indirectly, real-time-strategy games: it is a war scene viewed from above in miniature, but the fog of war is unbearably blown away.

Fucking Hell anchors World War II as the nexus for techno-futuristic fictional hell mutations, such as *Hellboy*, *Doom*, and the countless explorations of the Nazi occult. Once hell has boiled up to the surface, the purported ontological break between "beneath" and "elsewhere" is nullified as everything goes to hell in an exercise in Schellingian transcendental volcanism, erupting in plumes of hyper-chaos and hardening in accursed gems to power future weapons of planetary death.

5: TO CONCLUDE, OR, A DARK EARTH, A BLACK SUN

Great star! What would your happiness be, if you had not those for whom you shine! . . . I must descend into the depths: as you do at evening, when you go behind the sea and bring light to the underworld too, superabundant star!
  Nietzsche, *Thus Spoke Zarathustra*

One might equally denote this planet as the muddy planet, for it is the only one to be encased in a thick shell of mud and mudrock, being literally enveloped in its own decay products.
  Jan Zalasiewicz, *The Earth After Us*

5.1. DARK EARTH

Throughout Negarestani's *Cyclonopedia*, the possibility of a tellurian insurgency against the sun is posited, working in the vein of a Tiamaterialism, where the earth itself is taken up as a weapon against the solar empire.[147] The earth, as we have seen, does not require much labor to become a monster. The earth is a stratified globule, a festering confusion of internalities powered by a molten core and bombarded by an indifferent

---

[147]Negarestani, *Cyclonopedia*, 42.

star. This productive rottenness breeds the possibility of escaping the solar economy through the odd chemistry of ontology. The darkness of ground in Schelling, as Grant has argued, is a productive one.

The earth is "the dark ground of nature"[148] that attempts to create all on its own while always sinking back into a black chaos.[149] This odd and failed generation makes itself into immanent compost: "everything goes as into its ground; one ought rather to say: everything preceding grounded itself by the fact that it lowers itself to being the ground of what follows."[150] The ground of the earth constantly makes itself the ground of something else. Expanding the earth's productivity, Schelling writes:

> The abyss of forces down into which we gaze here opens up with the single question: in the *first* construction of our Earth, what can have been the ground of the fact that no genesis of new individuals is possible upon it, otherwise than under the condition of opposite powers?[151]

The earth must be a part of a larger system of forces, a system at the cosmic scale[152] in which the ground of the earth is the dark principal of night,[153] all of which, following Lorenz

---

[148] F.W.J. Schelling, *Philosophical Investigations into the Essence of Human Freedom*, trans. Jeff Love and Johannes Schmidt (Albany: State University of New York Press), 44.

[149] Schelling, *Philosophical Investigations*, 45.

[150] F.W.J. Schelling, *On the History of Modern Philosophy*, trans. Andrew Bowie (New York: Cambridge University Press, 1994), 158.

[151] Schelling, *The First Outline of a System,* 230.

[152] F.W.J. Schelling, *On University Studies*, trans. E. S. Morgan (Athens: Ohio University Press, 1965), 132.

[153] F.W.J. Schelling, *Idealism and the Endgame of Theory*, trans. Thomas Pfau (Albany: State University of New York Press, 1994), 217.

on an ungrounded earth | 85

Oken, lay in a chaotic yet stabilizing tension.[154] Furthermore, "The earth is the corporeal gravity, the substance as a perfectly simple position without emergence out of itself, the 0, the terrestrial monad."[155] Oken's failure in articulating the earth as a dark heavy zero (despite its genesis in crystallization) is in stating that it is only earth at its center. The complex immanence of the earth rests neither only at the core nor only on the surface. Deleuze and Guattari understand this when they write: "The earth is not one element among others but rather brings together all the elements within a single embrace."[156]

This geological immanence occurs at various depths. For Negarestani, oil, as a geopolitical lubricant, is the rotten corpse of the sun[157] that helps fuel the insurgency against the solar empire. This lubricant works with the ( )hole complex of the Earth as the first few components of the rotting earth move against the blazing star. This "degenerate wholeness" oscillates "between surface and depth—within solid matrices, fundamentally corrupting the latter's consolidation and wholeness through perforations and terminal porosities."[158] This ungrounded earth is, in a naturephilosophy without bodies, somewhat less peculiar. Engaging Land again: "Bodies are not volumes but coastlines; irresolvable but undelimitable penetrabilities, opportunities for the real decomposition of space."[159] And simply put, "Void excludes solidity, but solidity does not exclude void."[160]

In its most triumphant moments of assault, the Earth (along with nature's most terrible invention, thought) vomits

---

[154]Lorenz Oken, *Elements of Physiophilosophy* (London: The Ray Society, 1847), 41–43.
[155]Oken, *Elements of Physiophilosophy*, 89.
[156]Deleuze and Guattari, *What is Philosophy?* 85.
[157]Negarestani, *Cyclonopedia*, 12.
[158]Negarestani, *Cyclonopedia*, 43.
[159]Land, *The Thirst for Annihilation*, 161.
[160]Land, *The Thirst for Annihilation*, 164.

demons, pollutant clouds, and solar grubbing organisms as forced participation in, yet also secret resentment for, the Sun. Since the Earth cannot escape the Sun's orbit, it can only mutilate itself in the guise of cooperation. *Pace* Deleuze and Guattari, the Earth cannot merely swing between territory and non-territory—such swinging says nothing about its molten insider. Negarestani digs deeply on this point:

> Tellurian Insurgency does not merely run on oil and dust: A substantial part of it works with Cthellium and feeds on metal. The core (Cthelll), as a protrusive xenochemical insider, tries to induce violent anomalies in the Earth's body.[161]

But let us not forget that bodies themselves are completely envoided, swirlings of matter and forces, and, in a philosophical sense, messes of onto-epistemological indistinction. In terms of Schellingian transcendental geophilosophy, the transcendental is the surface and not the depths.[162] But if the transcendental is what makes the ideal into the real, it is not because the ideal has ontological priority but because our grasp of immanence is ideal since it never stops moving. The first force of nature would be endlessly productive if not for a second negative process.[163]

Earth as a storm of forces, as a darkly productive monster, seems far removed from the Earth discussed in ecology studies and in popular culture, where it is caught between a thing to be worshiped and a thing to be exploited, or as Pierre Hadot puts it, between the Orphic and the Promethean. The Earth is caught in a torrent of irreversible sludge as if all the pollution machines of all the Captain Planet villains were unleashed simultaneously and without end. The

---

[161] Negarestani, *Cyclonopedia*, 162.
[162] Grant, *Philosophies of Nature*, 205.
[163] See Iain Hamilton Grant, "Introduction to Schelling's *On the World Soul*," *COLLAPSE* VI: Geo/Philosophy (January 2010): 58–95.

irreversibility of this collapse, of this rotten-ness, is typically highly resisted.

It is a surprise that even in a cultural cloud as dark as that of Black Metal, the fantasy of complete ecological reversal remains. The central issue of Black Metal's inhumanity (or perhaps, the voiding of humanity proper) is the questionable place from which that void-loving misanthropy emerges, the core from which the disintegration of the human is loosed. Ecological Black Metal, such as that of the band Wolves in the Throne Room, indirectly highlights this problematic by narrowing the blackening of BM to target post-industrial inhumanity—positing a neo-pagan or otherwise earthly human as the proper inhuman subject to replace the contemporary capitalism-drenched being (a clear appeal to the Orphic tendency of thinking nature).

Such actions not only become increasingly indistinguishable from naive attempts at green thinking and ethics, but also require a presentation of the Earth as ordinary arche as well as a retention of the possibility of a miraculous reversibility of capitalist energetics—in the possibility of a purely earthly (non-artificial) production and form of life. The earth is always self-exteriorizing from our conceptions of it, via dramatic exteriorization (cosmological expansion) or via a horrifying deepening of its interiority (through the microbe, the viroid, and so forth), but this is ignored by Wolves in the Throne Room's project of setting out to "purify Black Metal" tout court in order to mirror their ecological view—stipulating not creation in the void of planetary destruction but a pre-Oedipal dream-harmony with nature.

It is with this invocation of Oedipus that we move to the great solar mother.

5.2. BLACK SUN

We see at a glance wide seas of fire, raising their

> flames towards the heavens, frantic storms, whose fury doubles the intensity of the burning seas, while they themselves make the fiery seas overflow their banks, sometimes covering the higher regions of this world body, sometimes allowing them to sink back down within their borders. Burned out rocks extend their frightening peaks up above the flaming chasms.
>
> Kant

> The sun is a whore.
>
> Daniel Schreber

Kant wants the sun to be a planet, badly. Hoping that the sun has an atmosphere of its own,[164] Kant praises the force of the sun, but this is only because he cannot stand the sun's distance. The philosopher's problem is that he wants to be the sun. At least Zarathustra is honest about it: "Thus spoke Zarathustra and left his cave, glowing and strong, like a morning sun emerging from behind dark mountains."[165] Judge Schreber took it a step further with the concept of the solar replenishment of his insides,[166] which allowed him to exist without organs, to be made only of sunbeams.[167] Deleuze and Guattari see this as a positive condition—Schreber's ability to attract sunbeams with his slippery body.[168]

---

[164] Kant, Immanuel, *Universal Natural History and Theory of the Heavens*, trans. Ian Johnston (Arlington: Richer Resources Publications, 2008), 107–108.

[165] Nietzsche, *Thus Spoke Zarathustra,* 336.

[166] Gilles Deleuze and Félix Guattari, *Anti-Oedipus: Capitalism and Schizophrenia*, trans. Robert Hurley, Mark Seem, and Helen R. Lane (Minneapolis: University of Minnesota Press, 1983), 2.

[167] Deleuze and Guattari, *Anti-Oedipus,* 8.

[168] Deleuze and Guattari, *Anti-Oedipus,* 15.

This is also the driving horror of Danny Boyle's *Sunshine*. In the film, a vessel is sent to the sun with a massive nuclear warhead in order to reignite the solar core. On the way, the crew experiences various problems—one goes sun-mad and spends more and more time in the viewing room, transfixed by the rage of the sun, before eventually allowing himself to be cooked alive. Another, while attempting to repair the sun, is overwhelmed by the cascading light of the sun and is killed. The crew eventually picks up a distress signal from the first ship, *Icarus I*, that attempted this mission, and they go aboard for repair materials. They soon learn that the captain of the first ship went sun-mad and, as a scorched piece of meat, he begins killing the remaining characters. True to the ship's name, the vessel is unable to withstand proximity to the sun, and it sacrifices itself in order to restart the sun, destroying the survivors in a blaze.

The sun is a destructive monster, yet its productive capacity cannot be overestimated. For Schelling, it is the chemical synthesizer of the earth,[169] as well as the imperfect

---

[169] Schelling, *First Outline of a System*, 88, 96.

hearth of the world that wishes to consume the earth.[170] Schelling describes the sun as a dynamic trigger this way: "External nature and earth would remain cold, dark, and completely secluded and devoid of creativity if they were not opposed by the effect of the sun."[171]

For Oken, it is also a strange gelatinous animal, an important creature in a totally organic cosmos.[172] For Negarestani, the sun is both vitalist and annihilationist in its empire over the earth.[173] What is required is a perverse immanent meld of the earth and the sun.[174] Furthermore, this sun-earth axis is the producer of hell from the black egg of the earth.[175]

Again it is tempting to return to Land and his pseudo-Bataillean naturephilosophy. The sun must be the illuminator for Plato and Socrates.[176] But there is, for Bataille, a second sun, a dark sun, a black sun:[177] "The sensations we drink from the black sun afflict us as ruinous passion, skewering our senses upon the drive to waste ourselves."[178]

There are strange dreams about surviving this aspect of the sun, which culminates in the cataclysm of its destruction preceded by its darkening, its blackening, and its degradation towards meltdown. In the closing pages of *Nihil Unbound*, Brassier writes:

> *Everything is dead already.* Solar death is catastrophic because it vitiates ontological temporality as configured in terms of philosophical ques-

---

[170]Schelling, *Bruno*, 175.
[171]Schelling, *Idealism and the Endgame of Theory*, 211.
[172]Oken, *Elements of Physiophilosophy*, 70.
[173]Negarestani, *Cyclonopedia*, 92.
[174]*Negarestani, Cyclonopedia*, 147.
[175]Negarestani, *Cyclonopedia*, 147.
[176]Land, *The Thirst for Annihilation*, 28.
[177]Land, *The Thirst for Annihilation*, 29.
[178]Land, *The Thirst for Annihilation*, 29.

tioning's constitutive horizonal relationship to the future. But far from lying in wait for us in the far distant future, on the other side of the terrestrial horizon, the solar catastrophe needs to be grasped as something that has already happened; as the aboriginal trauma driving the history of terrestrial life as an elaborately circuitous detour from stellar death.[179]

Two twisted conclusions resulting from this are an attempt to outlive the solar withering and the possibility of a dead and black sun. In the first instance, there is no better example than the work of William Hope Hodgson, and in particular *Night Land* and *The House on the Borderland*.[180] In the former, humanity cowers in a gigantic metal pyramid, watching the world mutate under the faded light of an extinct sun, whereas in the latter, the protagonist watches the universe and everything around him decay due to the ravages of time. In the second instance, we have the long cultic use of the black sun.

Goodrick-Clarke's text *Black Sun* provides a litany of interpretations of this occult phenomenon—from the alchemical *sol niger* as the first stage of creation, to Horbiger's black sun as a dark earth capturing planets, to Wiligut's black sun as an extinct star orbiting the earth, and finally to the black sun as the Babylonian inner light.[181] All the black suns form a vomitous circle of matter with the earth.

The figure of the black sun allows the earth to break out

---

[179]Ray Brassier, *Nihil Unbound: Enlightenment and Extinction* (New York: Palgrave Macmillan, 2007), 223.
[180]William Hope Hodgson, *The Night Land* (1912), Wikisource: http://en.wikisource.org/wiki/The_Night_Land, and *The House on the Borderland* (1908): http://en.wikisource.org/wiki/The_House_on_the_Borderland.
[181]Nicholas Goodrick-Clarke, *Black Sun: Aryan Cults, Esoteric Nazism, and the Politics of Identity* (New York: New York University Press, 2003), 131, 132, 147.

of its slavery, out of its baked mass, striking toward the sun or breaking away from it, before it boils the oceans away and kills all life on the planet. A black sun is the hope that the sun will rot and fall into the earth, and the dark earth is the wish that the planet will rocket, like a perforating monad, towards the sun—this is the dream of destroying it.

EXCURSUS: NIHILISMUS AUTODIDACTUS

And now at last the Earth was dead. The final pitiful survivor had perished. All the teeming billions; the slow aeons; the empires and civilizations of mankind were summed up in this poor twisted form—and how titanically meaningless it had all been! Now indeed had come an end and climax to all the efforts of humanity—how monstrous and incredible a climax in the eyes of those poor complacent fools in the prosperous days! Not ever again would the planet know the thunderous tramping of human millions—or even the crawling of lizards and the buzz of insects, for they, too, had gone. Now was come the reign of sapless branches and endless fields of tough grasses. Earth, like its cold, imperturbable moon, was given over to silence and blackness forever. The stars whirled on; the whole careless plan would continue for infinities unknown. This trivial end of a negligible episode mattered not to distant nebulae or to suns newborn, flourishing, and dying. The race of man, too puny and momentary to have a real function or purpose, was as if it had never existed. To such a conclusion the aeons of its farcically toilsome evolution had led.

H.P. Lovecraft, *Till A' the Seas*

We were too many. Such statements precede the evacuation of the earth due to overpopulation, a possibility all too possible, given the ongoing slumifiction and slime-ification of the capitalized earth.

There will be a great lesson in nihil: solar system after solar system will be found devoid of life. Sending von Neumann probes out into the void searching for the trace of life or even habitability will result in failures. That is, of course, if we can first escape not only the terrestrial but also the terrestrial as confining thought and life, as choosing a mode of living, of being unable to escape the storm of capitalist currents moving on the earth. In other words, we will only know that we are too many if we stop living as consumers.

One of the most unfortunate constants of science fiction is its humanistic optimism, whether secular or mythic. The unification of planets, of empires, and rebellions asserts a communitarian harmony as well as a ubiquity of civilized life. The post-apocalyptic and the dying earth subgenres offer some hope of desolation and pessimism but often relapse into pointless optimism. Leaving the Earth and the Sun behind means being open to the cosmos, beyond the possibility of being baked by the red and bloated sun as in Lovecraft's "Till A' the Seas," quoted above.[182] This openness does not inspire optimism, only dejection.

Beyond the nihilism of Michel Houellebecq's *The Possibility of an Island*,[183] where humanity's replacement functions plant-like under the sun, the sun must be left behind. The end of the solar economy opens the energetic economy toward total extinction. Extinction beyond the solar. Films like *Pandorum* and TV series such as *Battlestar Galactica* leave behind the sun, but all, unfortunately, find a

---

[182]H.P. Lovecraft, "Till A' the Seas," *The H.P. Lovecraft Archive*: http://www.hplovecraft.com/writings/fiction/tas.aspx.

[183]Michel Houellebecq, *The Possibility of an Island*, trans. Gavin Bowd (New York: Vintage, 2005).

home again. We must face the possibility that we will lose all sense of at-homeness.

We must cultivate a search for a new earth that ends in repeated failure, but in a sense that does not re-transcendentalize the original earth. Where the distress call leads to dead and empty vessels, where signs of life turn out to be no more than deadly microbes. A tale that ends only in the gradual thinning of the self-conscious biomass called humanity.

Bibliography

Alvanson, Kristen. "Elysian Space in the Middle East." *COLLAPSE* II: Speculative Realism (March 2007): 257–271.

Bennett, Jane. *The Enchantment of Modern Life: Attachments, Crossings, and Ethics.* Princeton: Princeton University Press, 2001.

Bennett, Jane. *Vibrant Matter: A Political Ecology of Things.* Durham: Duke University Press, 2010.

Bostrom, Nick. "Where Are They? Why I Hope the Search for Extraterrestrial Life Finds Nothing." *COLLAPSE* V: The Copernican Imperative (February 2009): 333–350.

Brassier, Ray. *Nihil Unbound: Enlightenment and Extinction.* New York: Palgrave Macmillan, 2007.

Brassier, Ray, Iain Hamilton Grant, Graham Harman, and Quentin Meillassoux. "Speculative Realism." *COLLAPSE* III: Speculative Realism (March 2007): 307–449.

Cirkovic, Milan. "Sailing the Archipelago." *COLLAPSE* V: The Copernican Imperative (February 2009): 294–332.

Dante. *The Divine Comedy, Volume I: Inferno,* trans. Mark Musa. London: Penguin Books, 1984.

De Landa, Manuel. *A Thousand Years of Nonlinear History.* New York: Zone Books, 2000.

Deleuze, Gilles. *Difference and Repetition,* trans. Paul Patton. New York: Columbia University Press, 1994.

Deleuze, Gilles, and Félix Guattari. *Anti-Oedipus: Capitalism and Schizophrenia,* trans. Robert Hurley, Mark Seem, and Helen R. Lane. Minneapolis: University of Minnesota Press, 1983.

Deleuze, Gilles, and Félix Guattari. *A Thousand Plateaus: Capitalism and Schizophrenia,* trans. Brian Massumi. Minneapolis: University of Minnesota Press, 1987.

Deleuze, Gilles, and Félix Guattari. *What is Philosophy?* trans. Hugh Tomlinson and Graham Burchell. New York: Columbia University Press, 1994.

Goodrick-Clarke, Nicholas. *Black Sun: Aryan Cults, Esoteric Nazism, and the Politics of Identity.* New York: New York University Press, 2003.

Grant, Iain Hamilton, "At the Mountains of Madness: The Demonology of the New Earth and the Politics of Becoming." In *Deleuze and Philosophy: The Difference Engineer,* ed. Keith Ansell Pearson, 93–114. New York: Routledge, 2000.

Grant, Iain Hamilton. "Being and Slime: The Mathematics of Protoplasm in Lorenz Oken's 'Physio-Philosophy'." *COLLAPSE* IV: Concept Horror (May 2008): 287–321.

Grant, Iain Hamilton. "Mining Conditions." In *The Speculative Turn: Continental Materialism and Realism*, eds. Levi Bryant, Nick Srnicek, and Graham Harman, 40–46. Melbourne: re.press, 2010.

Grant, Iain Hamilton. *Philosophies of Nature After Schelling*. London: Continuum, 2006.

Grant, Iain Hamilton. "Prospects for Post-Copernican Dogmatism: The Antinomies of Transcendental Naturalism." *COLLAPSE* V: The Copernican Imperative (February 2009): 415–454.

Guha, Manabrata. "Introduction to SIMADology: *Polemos* in the 21st Century." *COLLAPSE* VI: Geo/Philosophy (January 2010): 323–378.

Hägglund, Martin. *Radical Atheism: Derrida and the Time of Life*. Stanford: Stanford University Press, 2008.

Harman, Graham. *Guerrilla Metaphysics: Phenomenology and the Carpentry of Things*. Chicago: Open Court, 2005.

Harman, Graham. *Prince of Networks: Bruno Latour and Metaphysics*. Melbourne: re.press, 2009.

Harman, Graham. "Time, Space, Essence, and Eidos: A New Theory of Causation." *Cosmos and History: The Journal of Natural and Social Philosophy* 6.1 (2010): 1–17.

Hodgson, William Hope. *The House on the Borderland* (1908). *Wikisource*: http://en.wikisource.org/wiki/The_House_on_the_Borderland.

Hodgson, William Hope. *The Night Land* (1912). *Wikisource*: http://en.wikisource.org/wiki/The_Night_Land.

Houellebecq, Michel. *The Possibility of an Island,* trans. Gavin Bowd. New York: Vintage, 2007.

Kant, Immanuel. *Universal Natural History and Theory of the Heavens*, trans. Ian Johnston. Arlington: Richer Resources Publications, 2008.

Land, Nick. "Meat (or How to Kill Oedipus in Cyberspace)." *Body and Society* 1.3-4 (1995): 191–204.

Land, Nick. *Thirst for Annihilation: Georges Bataille and Virulent Nihilism*. New York: Routledge, 1990.

Latour, Bruno. *The Pasteurization of France,* trans. Alan Sheridan and John Law. Cambridge: Harvard University Press, 1988.

Ligotti, Thomas. "The Last Feast of the Harlequin." In *Grimscribe: His Lives and Works*, 3–48. New York: Jove Books, 1994.

Ligotti, Thomas. "The Sect of the Idiot." In *Songs of a Dead Dreamer*, 229–239. Burton: Subterranean Press, 2010.

Ligotti, Thomas, "Introduction." In Stuart Moore, Joe Harris, & alia, *The Nightmare Factory*. New York: Fox Atomic Comics, 2008.

Lovecraft, H.P. *The Fiction: Complete and Unabridged*, ed. S.T. Joshi. New York: Barnes and Noble, 2008.

Lovecraft, H.P. "Till A' the Seas." *The H.P. Lovecraft Archive*: http://www.hplovecraft.com/writings/fiction/tas.asp.

Long, Jeff. *The Descent*. New York: Jove Books, 2001.

Maimon, Salomon. *Essay on Transcendental Philosophy*. London: Continuum, 2010.

Manaugh, Geoff. *The BLDGBLOG Book*. San Francisco: Chronicle Books, 2009.

Masciandaro, Nicola. "Becoming Spice: Commentary as Geophilosophy." *COLLAPSE* VI: Geo/Philosophy (January 2010): 20–57.

Masciandaro, Nicola, ed. *Hideous Gnosis: Black Metal Theory Symposium I*. New York: CreateSpace, 2010.

Meillassoux, Quentin. *After Finitude: An Essay on the Necessity of Contingency*. London: Continuum, 2008.

Meillassoux, Quentin. "Subtraction and Contraction: Deleuze, Immanence, and Matter and Memory." *COLLAPSE* III: Unknown Deleuze (+ Speculative Realism) (November 2007): 63–107.

Merleau-Ponty, Maurice. *Nature: Course Notes from the College de France*. Evanston: Northwestern University Press, 2003.

Morton, Timothy. *The Ecological Thought*. Cambridge: Harvard University Press, 2010.

Morton, Timothy. *Realist Magic*. Ann Arbor: Open Humanities Press, 2013.

Negarestani, Reza. "The Corpse Bride: Thinking with *Nigredo*." *COLLAPSE* IV: Concept Horror (May 2008): 129–161.

Negarestani, Reza. *Cyclonopedia: Complicity with Anonymous Materials*. Melbourne: re.press, 2008.

Negarestani, Reza. "Memento Tabere: Reflections on Time and Putrefaction." *Eliminative Culinarism* [weblog], March 21, 2009: http://blog.urbanomic.com/cyclon/archives/2009/03/memento_tabi_re.html.

Negarestani, Reza. "Undercover Softness:An Introduction to the Architecture and Politics of Decay." *COLLAPSE* VI: Geo/Philosophy (January 2010): 379–430.

Nietzsche, Friedrich. *Thus Spoke* Zarathustra, trans. R.J. Hollingdale. London: Penguin Books, 2003.

Odenwald, Sten. *Patterns in the Void: Why Nothing is Important*. Boulder: Westview Press, 2002.

Oken, Lorenz. *Elements of Physiophilosophy*. London: The Ray Society, 1847.

Poe, Edgar Allen. "The Conqueror Worm." In *The Complete Works of Edgar Allan Poe: Vol. VII: Poems*, ed. James Albert Harrison (New York: Thomas Y. Crowell, 1902), 87–88.

Schelling, F.W.J. *On University Studies*, trans. E.S. Morgan. Athens: Ohio University Press, 1966.

Schelling, F.W.J. *Bruno: On the Natural and Divine Principle of Things*, trans. Michael G. Vater. Albany: State University of New York Press, 1984.

Schelling, F.W.J. *Idealism and the Endgame of Theory*, trans. Thomas Pfau. Albany: State University of New York Press, 1994.

Schelling, F.W.J. *On the History of Modern Philosophy*, trans. Andrew Bowie. Cambridge: Cambridge University Press, 1994.

Schelling, F.W.J. *First Outline of a System of the Philosophy of Nature*, trans. Keith R. Peterson. Albany: State University of New York Press, 2004.

Schelling, F.W.J. *Philosophical Investigations into the Essence of Human Freedom*, trans. Jeff Love and Johannes Schmidt. Albany: State University of New York Press, 2007.

Schelling, F.W.J. *The Grounding of Positive Philosophy*, trans. Bruce Matthews. Albany: State University of New York Press, 2007.

Schirmacher, Wolfgang. "Technoculture and Life Technique." In *Just Living: Philosophy in Artificial Life*. New York: Atropos Press (forthcoming).

Turner, Alice K. *The History of Hell*. New York: Mariner Books, 1995.

Verne, Jules. *Journey to the Center of the Earth*. New York: Bantam Books, 2006.

Zalasiewicz, Jan. *The Earth After Us: What Legacy Will Humans Leave in the Rocks?* Oxford: Oxford University Press, 2008.

Zielinksi, Siegfred. *Deep Time of the Media: Toward an Archeology of Seeing and Hearing by Technical Means*. New York: MIT Press, 2006.

Zoellner, Tom. *Uranium: War, Energy, and the Rock that Shaped the World*. New York: Viking Press, 2009.

www.ingramcontent.com/pod-product-compliance
Lightning Source LLC
Chambersburg PA
CBHW070939180426
43192CB00039B/2349